Francis A. Drexel
LIBRARY

Books For College Libraries
Third Edition

Core Collection

CHINESE LABOR IN CALIFORNIA, 1850-1880

An Economic Study

by

Ping Chiu

THE STATE HISTORICAL SOCIETY OF WISCONSIN

for

THE DEPARTMENT OF HISTORY, UNIVERSITY OF WISCONSIN

MADISON
1967

CONTENTS

LIST OF TABLES

ACKNOWLEDGMENT

The author wishes to express his profound indebtedness to Professor Vernon Carstensen of the University of Wisconsin for his unfailing guidance and encouragement, and to his colleague Professor Margaret Donovan for her painstaking and thorough editing. Any error in fact or judgment, any defect in reasoning, presentation, or style, however, are entirely his own. Not all suggestions were taken into consideration or acted upon. Acknowledgment would also not be complete without an expression of appreciation to the librarians and staffs of the Baker Library, The California Historical Society Library, the California State Library, the University of California Library, the Huntington Library, the Library of Congress, the Los Angeles Public Library, the Los Angeles Museum, the National Archives, the San Francisco Bureau of Mines Library, the San Francisco Public Library, the M. H. De Young Museum, the Stanford University Library, the Stanford Graduate School of Business Library, the library of the University of California at Los Angeles, the Wells Fargo Museum, the Wisconsin Historical Society, the University of Wisconsin Memorial Library, and the appropriate county officials in Los Angeles, San Joaquin, Sacramento, and Yuba counties of California for their courtesy and assistance.

INTRODUCTION

This study is an attempt to describe and analyze the role of Chinese immigrants within the framework of the general economic development of California. Emphasis is placed upon the timing of their entry and exit, the wage level, and the numbers or the percentage of Chinese in the major industries, together with their relation to the changing regional and national economy in the period 1848-1880. The "contributions" of the Chinese are implied in the general description of their economic activities; the discrimination against them is discussed in conjunction with the economic development of the state. Neither is the focus of this study.

Many historical writings concerning the problem of Chinese immigration have been written, primarily to influence opinions, social actions, and government legislation. Efforts to achieve a clear-cut delineation between facts, inferences, deduction, or personal opinion are, however, not numerous. An effort has been made, however, to incorporate only factual information in the present work. Views and opinions on the economic effects of Chinese labor are summarized in the last chapter with a brief appraisal. Social, political, religious, and moral arguments, important as they may be, are left out altogether. Precise data is not available in adequate detail and no attempt has been made to establish statistical correlations between factors, such as price, wage, profit, interest rates, and volume of imports, etc., or to fix their precise order of importance in causal explanation. Material in Chinese language offers few relevant economic data that can not be documented from other sources. Therefore, its inclusion would serve no useful purpose here.

The development of the economy of California within the years 1848-1880 can be divided into two major phases. The first, 1848-1867, was concerned chiefly with the predominance of mining, the strong inflationary pressure in 1848-1853, the subsequent deflationary trend, and the accompanying business instability and violent fluctuations. California constituted a distinct economic region during this period. High personal income and high transportation costs impeded the process of equalization of price and wage levels between California and the rest of the nation.

From 1843 to 1853 individual mining with its high labor input, high income and high mobility dominated the economy. Between 1854 and 1864, in a period of rapidly declining gold production, company mining gained ascendancy. With the rise of company mining, the industry became capital intensive, thus requiring large capital investment but a relatively small labor force. Subsequently the greater part of the white miners left or were reduced to menial mine labor. After 1865 gold production was stabilized, and mining came to be dominated by a few large companies.

During this period (1848-1867), the Chinese were mainly independent miners. The first wave of Chinese immigration and mass entry into mining occurred in 1852-1854. Subsequently this movement was checked by the combined forces of the decline of surface mining and the anti-Chinese riots, but Chinese immigration reached another peak between 1860 and 1863, a period preceded by the exodus of white miners. The late 1850's and early 1860's are conspicuous for their absence of anti-Chinese agitations.

After 1863 a large portion of the surface mines were worked out, and about ten thousand Chinese left the mines in the next five years. Some returned to China (between 1864 and 1867 there was a net loss of Chinese population in the United States); others found employment in San Francisco's woolen mills and cigar "factories," or in the rural areas as agricultural laborers. The majority of Chinese ex-miners, however, worked on the Central Pacific Railroad. In short, the study discerns that the unemployed or under-employed Chinese miners formed the main source of labor force for California's economic growth. Chapters one to four deal with the Chinese in this initial phase of California's economic development, with special emphasis on mining and railroads.

The second stage of economic growth in California, 1867-1880, is characterized by the expansion of agriculture, the rise of manufacturing industries, the integration of the state into the national economy and the protracted depression of the seventies. The Chinese immigrants were attracted to the rapidly developing job opportunities in agriculture, industry, and construction projects between 1868 and 1876. Already by the mid-1870's, the development of agriculture was affected by declining price and mounting costs, and the mushrooming sweatshop industries faced with intense Eastern competition. The final years of the second period witnessed recurrent, intense anti-Chinese riots. Chapters four to seven analyze the changing economic structure of California, the development of woolen, shoe, cigar, and clothing industries, and their relationships to the Chinese labor force.

As depression persisted in California the great debate on political economy began. Employers and their spokesmen maintained that business failures and unemployment were the logical consequences of regional high wage rates. A large number of observers, however, tended to agree with the employees' assertion that the competition of the Chinese was the primary cause of declining wage and employment. The relative merits of these arguments are evaluated in chapter eight.

Contemporary observers tended to assume there was but one single labor market in California, and that there was perfect labor mobility. The employers were the outstanding exception. But in fact, there were several labor markets co-existing in time and space. Each was relatively insulated from income and job competition of the others. The Chinese labor was concentrated in the low-price, low-wage fields, primarily in agriculture and import-competing industries. The majority of the white workers were in the high-price, high-wage fields and in non-import-competing industries.

For most of the import-competing industries in California, economic difficulties lay in the inability of local sweatshops to meet the price competition of products from the Eastern factories. Competition from the Chinese was only of secondary importance. As for the workers and shops in the high price or custom trades, these were the victims of a long-run shift to the mass-produced and mass-distributed goods, the high income elasticity of demand (an example of this latter factor was the demand for high priced goods which fluctuate immensely with a relatively slight change in income). Again Chinese labor was no more than a minor contributing factor to hardship on this level.

In the late 1870's, as in the case of 1867, workers whose jobs or wage rates were in no way affected by Chinese competition—such as teamsters, carpenters, masons—took over the leadership in the anti-Chinese movement. The expulsion of the Chinese was no longer a specific means to increase job opportunities for all Caucasians. It was regarded as a cure-all for all economic and social problems in California. Subsequently, the Chinese in California increasingly left the fields in which they competed with white workers. By 1890 economic conflicts between the races were reduced to a minimum. However, whenever the American myth of unlimited opportunity for each and every individual needed reassurance, the mere presence of the Chinese in the state offered a ready explanation for the gap between ideal and actuality. It might not be an intelligent or well-founded explanation, but it satisfied deep emotional requirements even as it vouched for the adequacy of the American dream.

CHAPTER I

THE GENERAL BACKGROUND OF CALIFORNIA, 1848-1859

The most important aspect of the history of early American California is the fact that within one decade the economy of the state went through two transitional periods. The first, the emergence of the mining industry was, by far the most spectacular and it has been the focus of a considerable body of historical writing. The second period, the maturity of the mining industry, being more prosaic in its developments and perhaps less over-powering in its imprint upon other regions, has so far received scant notice from scholars, though its impact on the state and its people was hardly less far-reaching. The focus of this study will be upon the latter.

In a sense every age is "transitional," with its social, economic, and political forms in process of change and re-integration, and with the shifting of power from one group to another, or from one region to the other. However, the special emphasis on the transitional nature of the California economy in these early days can be particularly justified by the quality of such changes. It is more than obvious that the sudden transformation of a pastoral, semi-isolated region to a role as one of the world's mining centers and commercial hubs was so profound that there was little in common between the old order and the new that was in process of taking definite form. It was no less true that the change-over from an individualistic, labor-intensive, mining industry to a corporate, capital-intensive one, demanded a corresponding social and economic readjustment. Though less spectacular, this might also be infinitely more agonizing for the many whom it directly involved or affected. Elements of similarity between

1

the old and the new often serve as a cushion to the shocks of change. But unfortunately there was little comfortable continuity in either period in California. The rapidity with which both transitions had taken place could not but aggravate the disruptive nature of the change.

This is especially true because mining dominated California's economy in the period of 1848-1867. Mining provided the largest single source of employment and investment, and other sectors of the economy were oriented primarily toward serving the mines and the miners. Wages and profits were usually high in frontier areas, but they were especially high on the mining frontier. In California during this period, wages tended to approximate the earnings of individual miners, and the interest rates reflected the investment returns of the mines. Consequently, during the years 1848-1853, the high income of the miners and the enormous profits of the mines brought about a strong inflationary trend. After 1853, as rich surface mines became scarce, profits, incomes, wages, and prices fell rapidly.[1] Various enterprises were established during this era for the sole purpose of serving mining and miners. These establishments could not be operated profitably on any other basis. Since pre-emption of high price markets had been their primary concern, the owners of such businesses established, financed, and often ran their establishments at much higher costs—(interest, raw materials, waste)—than could be justified by subsequent conditions.

The strong deflationary trend after 1853 placed these enterprises in a very precarious condition. With the passage of time, the gap between their original capitalization and the current market value became larger and larger, and the overhead charges, including interest charges on original investments, more and more oppressive. Hence, the relative competitive position in relation to newcomers worsened. Many of the business failures during this time were caused by this strong downward trend.

In addition, business during the early American period depended on the delicate balance between the levels of gold production, the close approximation of the total purchasing power, and the volume of import. The high prices of 1848 and 1849, following the discovery of gold near Sacramento for example, induced a spectacular increase in imports. This resulted in a market glut in 1850 and 1851. In the early part of 1852, Eastern merchants consequently reduced their con - signment. This reduction of imports unfortunately coincided with a record year of gold production. Prices climbed rapidly in late 1852 and remained at a high level throughout 1853. High prices again induced heavy import at a time when gold production already passed its peak. Glutted markets and bankruptcies followed in 1854.[2]

The intricate relations between rain, mining activity, and trade in the interior were even more unpredictable. For ex- ample, rainfall during 1849-1850 was heavy and transporta- tion between the mines and the major trading centers was greatly impaired. While provisions were sold at fabulous prices at the mines, Sacramento suffered from stagnation and unemployment. Anticipating another wet season, Sacramento merchants shipped large amounts of goods to the interior towns in advance. But during the 1850-1851 season, rainfall was light. Roads to the mines were open to the free movement of consumer goods. Even worse, the scarcity of water greatly reduced the production of gold and the purchasing power of the miners was also reduced. Consequently, Sacramento merchants sold out their merchandise at ruinous sacrifices.[3] In other words, errors of judgment or faulty predictions were fatal in the rapidly changing economy of California in the 1850's.

Gold mining also created serious problems in local labor supply. In the gold rushes which followed every discovery of a minor site people of all trades became miners. When the rush was over, they drifted back to the cities and towns. This had the effect of inflating the wage rate when mining was good, and of depressing the wage rate when the income of the surface miner was low. Labor turnover, therefore, was extremely high and the labor market was inordinately unstable though the number of wage laborers available at any given instance was decidedly trifling.

In another area changes in mining technology culminated in the triumph of company mining and brought about a certain

moderating influence to the business community. This was
reflected in the decline of the bankruptcy suits: [4]

TABLE 1

BANKRUPTCY SUITS, 1855-1860

Date	No. of suits	Debts	Assets	Deficits
1855	197	$8, 317, 827	$1,519, 175	$6, 838, 652
1856	146	3, 401, 042	657, 908	2, 743, 134
1857	125	2, 375, 899	812, 417	2, 281, 880
1858	96	1, 940, 662	658, 782	1, 281, 880
1859	60	706, 219	208, 044	498, 157
1860	68	1, 019, 410	76, 787	942, 629

As the region became settled, it became less easy to take
advantage of bankruptcy laws because of public and private
sanctions. The decline in bankruptcy suits does not however,
necessarily imply a comparable growth in business stability.
Evidence of this is to be seen in the business mortality rates
compiled in the San Francisco Directories for the years 1860-
1868. This is reproduced in the following table:[5] An annual
business mortality rate of 30 to 39% was frightening indeed,
but according to the compiler of the directories, Henry G.
Langley, the yearly turnover of smaller firms not included in
his tabulation would not fall short of 50%. [6] Even though
business turnover was by no means synonymous with business failures in a rapidly changing economy, the need for
additional stabilizing forces could not escape the leaders of
the business community.

    If these technological changes and the rise of company
mining provided the business community with a certain degree
of stability it badly needed, the effect upon the individual
miners was overwhelmingly disruptive. In the very beginning
of the Gold Rush, in 1848 and early 1849, the most crude and

TABLE 2

BUSINESS MORTALITY RATES IN SAN FRANCISCO, 1860-1868

Number of Firms	Date	Failed in Business	Remained in Business
4,155	1860	1,556	2,599
4,911	1861	1,885	3,106
5,300	1862	1,880	3,420
no report	1863		
6,033	1864	1,869	4,176
no report	1865		
6,573	1866	2,617	3,956
6,942	1867	2,243	4,659
7,460	1868	2,233	5,228

common implements such as pick and shovel had been adequate for successful gold mining.[7]   With the exhaustion of the rich surface deposits, it became necessary to penetrate deeper into the ground and to wash larger amounts of "dirt" to realize what was considered a fair return.   To meet the technical need a series of innovations in mining methods took place.   These began in 1848 with the rocker, through 1850 with the long tom, followed in the same year by the sluice and the flume, and finally the even more efficient quartz and hydraulic mining of 1851 and 1852.[8] Technical innovations continued to appear through the period 1850-1880, especially in the field of hydraulic mining.   Judged from the continuity of operation and profit, company mining might be considered as having reached maturity about 1858.

In conjunction with these innovations came the systems of sinking shafts and driving tunnels for bed rock deposits. Water could no longer be taken as it came, but had to be brought in a stream to the mines. As the deposits near natural water-ways were exhausted, ditches were dug, some of great length and elaboration. Henceforth water acquired a market value, so much per miner's inch. Water and canal companies became an important branch of the mining industry, employing a great number of people and controlling the livelihood of many more.

Technical changes demanded certain social adjustments. Pick and shovel were used for individualistic operation, the rocker made possible and desirable the co-operation of two or three people, long toms required three to five men, sluices five to twenty, and flumes twenty or more.[9] With the ascendency of quartz and hydraulic mining, what once had been an individualistic undertaking became a business enterprise. Capital investment, management innovation, and the employment of a large number of wage earners were required. Technology set the pace and the rhythm that men were forced to live by. Though many pioneer miners rebelled, machinery and its resulting institutions persisted as the mining industry matured.

During the early period of the Gold Rush, every person could hope to enjoy for himself the prospect of success. Each aspired to be a prospector, anticipating bigger and better finds. In fact, some writers have asserted that the early miners spent more time in seeking new discoveries than in working their claims.[10] However, eagerness, enthusiasm, and confidence were not supported by the knowledge, training, equipment or capital required to guarantee a fair chance of success. Many disappointments stemmed from poor or inadequate prospecting. Seemingly rich claims were often quickly exhausted, others might require considerable capital to operate. Miners and observers alike tended to equate mining with a lottery, but in reality the underlying cause of much of the uncertainty in placer mining lay much deeper than pure luck or chance.

Before 1853 or so, though mining and prospecting were indeed hazardous, all men seemed to take the same degree of risk. As mining was converted into a business enterprise, becoming gradually larger and more expensive, it required sustained work and investment before results could be expected. The risks undertaken by the individual miner, either as operator or prospector, became progressively out of proportion with the rewards.   Large companies, commanding the services of geologists and metallurgists, could at least minimize the numerous hazards that plagued so many "independents". By controlling various subsidiary organizations, such as quartz mills or water and canal companies, the mining corporations could spread their risks and exploit users of such services, who were usually the independent miners. In other words, as time went on the pioneer miner-prospector found it harder and harder to compete successfully, or even to survive.

The year 1853 has been cited as the turning point accounting for the extinction of the enterprising miner-prospectors.[11] Significantly, it was in 1853 that the California legislature passed a joint resolution authorizing a geological survey at the expense of the state. Subsequently a report was issued[12] which afforded an official recognition of the passing of an amateur prospecting era. Again it was in 1853 that a strong deflationary trend began.   The era of high income for independent miners was over.

Technological advances, by reducing the costs per unit of raw material handled, extended work progressively to comparatively low grade mines. According to contemporary estimates, the rocker was five times as efficient as the pick, the long tom gained as much upon the rocker, and the saving effected by the sluice was found to be three-fold over the tom; finally, hydraulic mining reduced the costs of extraction of gold to less than a cent per cubic yard of gravel or one and one-fourth cents to eight cents per ton, while under the old rocker it would be $5.00 per cubic yard, assuming wages at $4.00 per day.[13]

In the beginning such innovations were a blessing to all, since they opened up new opportunities. They also led to an increase in the size of the mining claims. Even the size of the surface claims grew from ten to twenty feet water frontage to 100 or 200 feet.[4] Thus "elbow room" with its economic opportunity so preciously treasured by the pioneer miners, disappeared without warning.

Technical improvement also made possible reworking of mining claims for the gold that cruder methods of previous

owners had failed to extract. When the pioneer miners re-
traced their steps, searching claims to rework instead of
prospecting for virgin soil, their resentment toward the Chinese
who had taken up their abandoned claims and worked them
"profitably," turned into hostility. By this time, the Chinese
were regarded as serious competitors. They no longer could
be tolerated.

Concurrently with the intensification of competition for
surface mining claims occurred a downward trend in the miner's
income. In working low-grade mines, or reworking the old
ones, the improved mining tools and machineries increased
only the quantity of gravel treated but not necessarily the
amount of gold produced per person or per certain amount of
capital investment. In other words, the marginal product of
capital or labor often remained constant, or decreased, rapid
advancement in technology notwithstanding. With a rise in
investment but no corresponding gain in output, a substantial
decline in the rates of return upon capital as well as labor
was inevitable.

In addition to a downward adjustment in their income, the
pioneer miners also lost their status as independent producers,
as mining and water and canal companies gained ascendancy.
It was under these circumstances the first wave of the anti-
Chinese movement took shape.

In the fifties anti-Chinese sentiments were limited primarily to the mining districts. The merchants of San Francisco, as well as those of the interior towns, were keenly
aware of the importance of the Chinese as consumers. Per
capita spending of the Chinese might be much lower than that
of the white miners, but its aggregate was considerable.
Their habits of paying cash and honoring debts contributed
in no small measure to the welfare of the mercantile community during a period of violent and frequent business
fluctuations.

Thus the first alignments of "class interests" occurred.
On the one hand stood the miners who looked upon the Chinese
as competitors and as a contributing factor to the growth of
mining companies. On the other hand there were the traders,
who viewed the Chinese as consumers. The merchants in

turn were in alliance with the capitalists, who considered the Chinese chiefly as a potentially cheap labor force, which might be used in the rapid exploitation of California's rich resources. This division of interests prevailed through the 1850's.

After 1863, when the Chinese left the mines en masse, California for the first time in history had an abundant supply of labor. Between 1863 and 1867 however, the Central Pacific Railroad absorbed a major portion of this labor force. After 1867, numerous manufacturing industries and construction projects, such as irrigation and reclamation, were launched with Chinese labor. Farmers were provided with an adequate and dependable labor supply. The potential utilization of a large Chinese labor force for regional economic development became a reality. Henceforth, California's economy entered into a new stage of growth, and the Chinese wage labor became a leading subject of controversy within this broader social context.

CHAPTER II

IN THE MINES, 1849-1880

Part I: 1849-1857

Anti-foreign agitation in California was initially directed against those people from Latin American countries, who had preceded the Eastern immigrants, presumably had "preempted" some of the better mining claims, and perhaps were more successful in their mining operations because of previous experience. By June, 1850, the pressure on the legislature was so great that a foreign miner's tax of $20 per month was imposed.[1] The resulting exodus of foreign miners reached such a magnitude that in some communities people who had invested in real estate and trade were immediately alarmed. These interests secured repeal of the tax, reflecting the division of interests between the miners and the traders which would persist for years in California.[2] That division would later operate similarly over the Chinese issue.

The Chinese, few in number, late comers by comparison, inexperienced and working mostly on poorer claims, were on the whole tolerated in the mines. Here and there miners felt resentful when news reached them that the claims they had given up paid handsomely to some Chinese, while their own new adventures turned out to be no better than blighted hope. However, overt hostility was rare.

One of the most important sources on early California mining is J. D. Borthwick's Three Years in California. As far as the Chinese are concerned, this is perhaps the only book that offers more than anecdotes. One of the characteristics of the Chinese miners, according to Borthwick, was their almost

10

feminine way of handling tools, "As if they were afraid of
hurting themselves." Another was their aversion to working
in water or in heat, and their inability to work long hours under
such conditions without periodic rests.[3] The third was their
inexperience and inefficiency in handling mechanical devices,
although projects of considerable size and magnitude were
sometimes completed by them.[4] Their inexperience can easily
be understood and needs no commentary here. Their apparent
"inability" to work long hours can partially be explained by
the fact that it was an established custom for workers in
China to sit down and have tea in mid-afternoon. However,
the most distinguishable characteristic of the Chinese is the
fact that they did not venture to assert equal rights in taking
claims but were "content" to work on poor, $2 a day, claims.
However, if they had happened to strike a rich lead, they
would most probably have been immediately driven off.[5]

There was, in addition, a conspicuous lack of large Chinese
camps in the mining areas. The 1850 manuscript census recorded that the largest congregation in one district was ap-
proximately 23, averaging about three persons in each dwelling, with the exception of Sutter County, where the largest
group was 42 and averaged 15 per dwelling. The distribution
of Chinese in 1850 is shown in Table 3, according to that
source.[6]

TABLE 3

GEOGRAPHICAL AND OCCUPATIONAL DISTRIBUTIONS OF THE
CHINESE—1850

Counties	Occupations		
Calaveras	139 miners	10 merchants	1 baker
El Dorado	5 miners		
Los Angeles			1 servant
Sacramento	6 miners		2 laundrymen
Sutter	176 miners		
Tuolumne	18 miners	1 merchant	

Of the 57,787 miners in the state in 1850,[7] only some 500 were Chinese. They were indeed insignificant, if not inconspicuous. This corroborated the early Gold Rush observation that the Chinese preferred San Francisco and rarely went to the mines.[8]

The first incident of anti-Chinese rioting, according to Theodore Hittell, took place as early as 1849 at Chinese Camp, Tuolumne county. About 60 Chinese working for a British company under the supervision of some Sonorans were driven off the mine by a party of white miners. The claim reportedly paid well at the time; it was to remain unworked for some years but at a later period again yielded immense returns.[9] Regrettably no further information about this episode is available.

A copy of a blank contract between a British firm in Shanghai and an unknown number of Chinese is kept in the Wells Fargo Museum in San Francisco. In it, the British firm, in addition to offering employment in California, agreed to advance $125 as passage money, which was to be repaid in monthly deductions from the wages of the Chinese, under arrangement between the firm and their employer. The contract was drawn up in 1849, printed in both languages, English and Chinese, and was clearly designed to be signed by individual laborers. It was not to be handled through intermediary contractors. Unfortunately the number of laborers thus hired, their wages, and the amount of deductions are unknown. An American consul in Canton reported the same kind of arrangements in South China.[10] Again, however, definite information is lacking.

The Tuolumne expulsion episode is of interest to us in several respects. The first large scale anti-Chinese riot seems to have been directed against Chinese mining laborers. Their employers would be more competitive with the pioneer miner-prospectors than the individual Chinese miners themselves. Secondly, it took place at Tuolumne county, where the celebrated Columbia Resolution[11] was adopted three years later, in 1852. Thirdly, no similar incident against Chinese mining laborers occurred until the late 1860's. Thus this was the exception to the rule of Chinese independent mining being the main target of riots in the mines.

In the intervening three years, between the first riot and the first organized agitation, the change-over from individual to company mining was well on its way. As surface deposits close to natural waterways became scarce, the miners became more aware of their dependence upon the water and canal companies. At the same time quartz and hydraulic mining were proving their potential as profitable business enterprises. The "capitalists" pressing for the Tingley Bill, a law to enforce labor contracts drawn up abroad, touched off a bitter fight in the legislature in March, 1852. [12]

Up until 1852, population movement across the Pacific had been light. The most probable estimate was given by the San Francisco Custom Office, according to which the arrivals from China were 325 in 1849, 450 in 1850 and 2,700 in 1851. [13] Since part of the 1850 census was lost, including the all-important parts covering San Francisco, it is not possible to check the accuracy of those figures. However, before the end of 1852, 20,000 more Chinese were to arrive and the Chinese population in the state perhaps had grown five-fold in one year.

The sudden influx of 20,000 Chinese must have had an electrifying effect on the Californians. Coming coincidentally with the beginning of company mining, the immigration was especially odious in the eyes of the independent miner. This is especially so because the majority of the Chinese lived in predominantly American communities, as the 1852 manuscript census revealed. Almost one-third of the Chinese lived in large camps, and only a few hundred resided in localities with large foreign, non-Chinese population. [14] Therefore in the 1850's there had been few incidents of friction between the Chinese and other foreign immigrants, something that became commonplace in the 1870's.

The first important event that brought the problem of the Chinese to the foreground was Governor John Bigler's special message to the legislature on April 23, 1852. [15] The emphasis of the message was on the Chinese "coolie" (i.e. contract labor) in the state. The message might have been intended to kill the Tingley Bill introduced in March since the existing number of foreign wage laborers could not have been so large as to cause grave concern. It might also have been a vote-getting technique. Bigler was greeted by tumultuous applause in the mining counties on his tour, but he was branded as a demagogue by the "better elements" of the society.[16] A few days after the governor's message, the miners in Columbia, Tuolumne county, met and drew up a set of resolutions which later touched off a series of organized anti-Chinese riots in the state.

The big rush to the vicinity of Columbia had resumed in the summer of 1851, after the temporary set-back of 1850 on account of the Foreign Miner's Tax and the scarcity of water. Throughout late 1851 and early 1852 people were busy staking out claims, some for town lots, others for mining, in anticipation of the completion of the ditches of the Tuolumne County Water Company. Unexpected delays however, postponed the project's completion until late fall. In the meantime miners had no alternative but to wait. Drinking, gambling, brawling and fighting reduced the town to turmoil. Reminiscing in 1854, one settler found it almost unbelievable, especially in contrast with the peaceful and quiet community that it was to be two years later.[17] Under these circumstances the celebrated Columbia Miners' Convention met, on May 8, 1852.[18] The explicit objective of the convention and of its later resolutions was the expulsion of the Chinese from the mines in the vicinity of Columbia. The main theme in the argument was the willingness of the Chinese to work for low wages. Around this point other objections—social, religious, political, and economic—were elaborated. Here, however, the central theme alone is a matter of concern.

Wage was a loose term in those days. It could mean either wage or income, and the resolution failed to make any distinctions. Hence the statement could mean that the Chinese, contented with a lower income, were more willing to comply with the demands of the water company. If this was the case, the miners were anticipating the same grievances raised by miners in Gold Hill and Placerville.[19] However, the ditches were still under construction and the realization of high water rates in relation to the yield of gold from the claims was still a matter of the future. The miners might have some idea or knowledge about the water rates in other counties, or what the company was going to charge, but they could not have accurately calculated the yield before operation. Hence there seemed to be no cause for immediate alarm on this issue.

On the other hand it may mean that the Chinese were actually employed as laborers by the large companies at low wages. But there was no mining company of any size to speak of aside from the water company in the neighborhood. Quartz excitement had indeed hit Tuolumne County in 1851, but it was of a much lesser magnitude compared to the excitement aroused in the northern counties.[20] Furthermore, if the mills or mines had been erected they must have failed in early 1852, for the census listed no mining companies or capital invested in such enterprises. (If the mills or mines failed after the Columbia Resolution a scant one month before the census taking, this would have been noted in the census or in the newspapers.) As for hydraulic mining, it was still in an experimental stage even in the North, the leading region in technical innovations. In addition to this, if the manuscript census can be trusted, few Chinese were hired as ditch diggers or tenders until 1870. In other words, the number of Chinese wage workers in the area must have been very small.

If the threat of Chinese competition was largely imaginary or remote, the miners' dependence upon the water company was real and current. All of the implications of the dependence might not have been fully realized at that moment; its gravity was nevertheless made evident by prolonged compulsory idleness due to the delay of the completion of the ditches. Therefore it is safe to assume that the convention and the resolution to expel the Chinese were motivated as much, if not more, by the miners' anxiety over their loss of status as independent operators, as by the fear of Chinese competition.

In fact, though it was not dealt with explicitly in the resolution, the Tuolumne County Water Company, estimated at a cost of $200,000 in the beginning of 1852,[21] must have loomed ominously in the minds of the independent miners. What was left unsaid in the resolutions might have been the hope that by banishing the docile Chinese the miners might be able to gain better bargaining power with the company, or that by excluding potential wage earners, presumably the Chinese, they might be able to reverse the trend toward company mining.

The miners' anti-capitalistic sentiments were not entirely suppressed in the resolution. One section contained a forceful condemnation of the selfishness of the "capitalists," the shipowners, and the merchants who profited by the transporting or the presence of the Chinese.[22] The division of interests first came to view in 1850 with the passage of the Foreign Miner's Tax, and was crystallized two years later.

The Chinese were driven from the vicinity of Columbia soon after passage of the resolution. However, after the Chinese were expelled and the ditches completed, the miners faced bitter disappointment. The water rates were anything but reasonable from their viewpoint. Many were compelled to abandon the claims they fought so hard to obtain and to preserve.[23] Similar circumstances existed in the nearby town of Sonora, with the same type of anti-Chinese meeting and the same losing battle against the giant water company.[24]

It is generally assumed that the organized anti-Chinese movement in the form of miners' conventions originated in Columbia, but actually it was preceded by one in Foster and Atchinson's Bar, Yuba county. It resolved that no Chinese should be allowed to hold mining claims after May 1, 1852, and none be allowed to remain in the area after May 3, 1852. A committee was formed to communicate the resolution to the Chinese, and copies of the proceeding were forwarded to newspapers in Marysville, Sacramento, and San Francisco.[25] Riots soon broke out,[26] and the Chinese were driven away.

In spite of the desire and the efforts of the participants to publicize their action, the Foster and Atchinson's Bar resolution and the subsequent riot did not capture the attention of the state and was soon forgotten. This obscurity was due in part to the failure of the resolution to make a declaration of principles. The resolution was simple, and direct to the point of stark nakedness. It gave no rationale, and put forward no moral, social, political, or economic arguments. It had, however, the misfortune of being followed within a few days by the Columbia convention which offered an explanation and justification.

The bone of contention in the Foster Bar area seemed to be mining claims which had direct access to natural waterways. According to Stephen Williams, who made a trip to the mines to locate the remains of these early Chinese camps, such sites were almost invariably situated on the bank of a river or its branches.[27] The Chinese mining claims, listed in the Calaveras mining laws from 1854 to 1857, as a rule had river frontage.[28] Thus, if the white miners sought to maintain their independence either from the mining or the water companies, they came into conflict with the Chinese over the river claims.

Thus two prototypes of anti-Chinese conventions were set early in 1852. The Columbia type later took the form of organized anti-Chinese movements in which anti-Chinese and anti-capitalistic sentiments were intrinsically involved. The other type, though numerically more significant, was sporadic, uncoordinated, and without ideological appeal. It was to be absorbed by the first type in the late 1860's and 1870's.

At the time these conventions met, a committee was formed to report on the governor's special message on Asiatic immigration.[29] Soon the Committee on Mines and Mining interests took over the investigation and broadened its scope. Subsequently three reports were issued.[30] The opinions of the committee members were as divided as the varying economic interests in the state.

The majority report and one of two minority reports, confident of the superiority of the Anglo-Saxon race, discounted the seriousness of Chinese competition or the danger of being overrun by the Chinese. Stressing the importance of the China trade, these reports perhaps spoke for the commercial interests.[31] The San Francisco merchants deplored the undue alarm and the amount of political demagoguery about the Chinese issue in the interior. They were not alone in this, for on the same day of the Columbia convention the Nevada City (California) Journal published in the center of the mining district, printed a letter signed "a merchant" from the nearby Rough and Ready. He stated his objections to the Foreign Miner's Tax, advocated a liberal immigration policy, and asserted: "It is doubtful whether the English and French immigrants coming directly from their countries will do more for California than the Chinese.[32]

By contrast, the other minority report reflected more closely the sentiments at Columbia and other mining districts,
stating: "We cannot raise these hirelings to our equality,
but must sink to their level; the dignity of honest toil has
gone...."[33] In other words, with the exhaustion of rich surface mines, and the ascendency of company mining, the independent miners looked at the fate of wage-earners with
bewilderment, apprehension and anxiety. They were convinced
that the exclusion of the Chinese was a means to arrest the
growth of the companies.

Because of conflicting interests aroused over the issue,
the state government limited itself to tax legislation. in 1852
a tax of $3 per month was imposed on foreign miners and em-
ployers were made responsible for its payment.[34] In 1853 an
amendment raised the tax to $4 per month and the tax collec-
tors were authorized to seize and sell the property of those
who failed to pay.[35] In the following year another law was
passed raising the tax by $2 at every two-year interval; this
act was repealed before it became effective.[36] At this time
the Foreign Miner's Tax was synonymous to the Chinese
miners' tax, since persons who had shown "the desire" to
become permanent residents were exempted from such burdens.
The attempt to prevent Chinese immigration by taxing the
shipowners was never successful even though a law to attain
this end was passed and stayed on the statute books for a
brief period.[37]

The arrival of some 16,000 Chinese in 1854 touched off
another wave of anti-Chinese agitation. This started in February,1855,with the Shasta County miners' convention, which
failed to win a sympathetic hearing from the special legislative committee. Both the majority and the minority reports
stressed the importance of California's economic growth, and
in their opinion Chinese immigrants appeared certain to further
the development of natural resources that might otherwise
remain dormant.[38]

The situation in Shasta county in 1855 was comparable to
that in Tuolumne county three years earlier. The gold rush
began in 1853 at the news of new discoveries and projected
mining ditches. The anti-Chinese convention took place on

February 25, 1855, coinciding with the completion of the Clear Creek Ditch.[39] As in the case of the Columbia conven-tion, expulsion of the Chinese from the district failed to deal with the basic problems. Thus in 1856 and 1857 mining was described as "ruinous."[40]

After the passage of the resolution, the majority of the Chinese left Shasta County for other localities or went into other employment, but a few remained. A group of white miners agreed to protect them for a fee.[41] Such arrangements might have been in existence as early as 1856, for in that year a number of Chinese brought suit to recover their claims from a group of white intruders. The jury, composed of 12 white miners, decided in their favor and as a result they were rein-stated. Soon afterwards, they were again driven off; again they claimed the protection of the law and the offenders were arrested.[42] Again, in Mokelumne Hill, Calaveras county, a group of Chinese spent $70,000 for the purchase of the mining sites and freedom from molestation.[43] This might suggest that the protection "rackets" were not isolated phenomena.

However, the evictions of Chinese may not imply unanimity of opinion among the miners. The expulsion of the Chinese from Drytown, by a resolution passed in a miners' meeting by a slim majority of 23 to 20,[44] exemplifies another issue. There the main complaint against the Chinese was the allega-tion that their presence depressed the prevailing wage scale. As previously indicated, during the early 1850's wages tended to conform with the income level of the independent miners. When mining was prosperous, people flocked to the mines, causing a labor shortage in the cities and on the farms, thus raising the wage scale. When the rush was over, many drifted back to town and the wage scale declined. Both income and wages showed a strong downward trend during this period. Toward the end of the 1850's there were clear indications that wages of skilled laborers , including mining laborers, ex-ceeded the income of the independent miners. This was an-other evidence that the age of pioneer mining was a thing of the past. Rodman W. Paul compiled a table on wages (income), which is reproduced on the following pages.[45]

Even for the skilled, wage scales were fluid during this

TABLE 4

WAGE RATES, 1848-1858

Date	Miners' Income— Wages	Wages from Other Sources
1848	$20	
1849	16	$12
1850	10	$ 5-8
1851	8	
1852	6	6
1853	5	skilled $6-8 unskilled $4.5
1856-58	3	skilled $4.5-5 unskilled $3

period. There were also substantial regional or local differences and any figures given are necessarily suggestive in nature. The wage listings shown in Table 5 are taken from a fair sized, 24 stamp, quartz mill, with a capacity of 300 tons per week.[46] The figures reflect the perhaps typical variance.

In contrast with wages, there was little change in the price of wood and oil for fuel; of the $27 reduction in daily operating cost, only $5 represented savings from price in raw materials. Wages for mining laborers showed the same trend, the pay for skilled and unskilled $7 and $5 respectively in 1853, and $4 and $3 in 1856.[47]

TABLE 5

WAGE RATES IN A MEDIUM SIZE QUARTZ MILL, 1853, 1856

Job Classification	1853	1856
Foreman	$7	$5
Engineer	8	5
Feeders	4.5	3
Men on Platform	6	4.5
Amalgamator	6	4.5
Carpenter	7	5

There is evidence pointing to the fact that the reduction of wages came in late 1854 or early 1855. In estimating the costs for operating a quartz mill in 1855, the San Francisco Bulletin put down the monthly wages for engineers at $150, blacksmiths and carpenters at $150, and laborers at $80. [48] Except for the unskilled, the wage scale was substantially the same as the one we have given for 1856. It is important to note that this substantial reduction in wages was preceded by heavy immigration from China in 1854, and coincided with the second wave of anti-Chinese agitation.

The exact extent of influence that the Chinese exerted on the downward trend of wages can never be determined. It cannot be isolated from other factors. After the inflationary forces of the first few years of the Gold Rush had spent themselves, there was a strong deflationary trend of prices as well as wages. Moreover, the process of equalization of factor price should not be overlooked. In the long run, California's wage levels would approach those of the United States' average, unless surface mines were inexhaustibly rich or it could be assumed that California could bar white as well as Chinese immigration completely. Furthermore, in the 1850's few Chinese were wage laborers, hence the effect of Chinese labor on wages was negligible.

What apparently most exasperated the independent miner was the fact that the wage of the unskilled laborer declined faster than that of the skilled laborer although company mining had proved its potentialities. This meant that the pioneer miners lost their status as independent operators, and in addition, the longer they waited to make the transition from owner-operators to wage earners the greater the gap between the skilled and unskilled became. Starting from the bottom of the ladder was not exactly what they hoped for when they left the East. Given a certain size of claim, the net income of the independent miner depended on the costs (water rates, tools, implements, machinery, etc.) and the quantity of the final product. That, in turn, depended on the quality of the mining site, and not on the competition of the Chinese.

One other topic must be investigated: the total number of the Chinese in California and their dispersion. Unfortunately, in spite of the amount of literature written about the Chinese, we have little actual evidence. There are insurmountable difficulties even in securing estimates of the total number of Chinese in the state as a whole on a yearly basis. Discrepancies often exist between the immigration figures and census figures. Data on annual immigration are reproduced in Appendix Three.   Imperfect as they are, these data represent the best available.

As we have pointed out earlier, the influx of Chinese in the years 1852 and 1854 caused immediate agitation and riots. These resulted in a sudden drop of net immigration in the following years. But from 1856 to 1859 the population flow from China was fairly stable. The sudden increase in 1860 was probably a direct result of the mass exodus of white miners in 1859 and thereafter, a fact that will be dealt with   extensively in the next section.

The dispersions of the Chinese by each county is even harder to determine. The best index for the internal migration of the Chinese miners is perhaps the yearly receipts of the Foreign Miner's Tax. Even here the amplitude of the fluctuation is perhaps exaggerated by the difficulties of collection during depression. Because of the relative stability in mining in the period 1854-1858, this built-in bias is perhaps less significant than the next period, 1859-1865. The pattern of population fluctuation for each county might or might not conform with that of the state as a whole. Often it was of a much greater magnitude.   Table 6 gives the receipts of the major mining counties   and that of the state. [49]

The drastic downward trend in Calaveras, the strong upward trend in Placer and Tuolumne, and violent fluctuations in Mariposa are the most noticeable deviations from that of the state as a whole.   Regrettably, a comparable table for white miners cannot be compiled for lack of data, nor even for the white population as a whole because of the inefficiency in the collection of poll taxes.

The organizational nature of the large Chinese camps in 1852 is also subject to much conjecture and controversy as to whether they were production units or simply residential units. One of the few mining claim records in existence is

TABLE 6

FOREIGN MINER'S TAX RECEIPTS, 1854-1858

Counties	1854	1855	1856	1857	1858
Amador		$ 3,227	$10,000	$ 8,805	$14,861
Butte	$ 3,343	4,680	16,614	14,516	18,312
Calaveras	20,543	14,547	6,624	8,303	1,185
El Dorado	28,953	22,460	42,517	28,297	21,339
Mariposa	7,192	4,893	20,045	5,809	13,268
Nevada	9,688	14,369	16,049	11,303	3,769
Placer	11,036	12,477	16,075	19,198	14,702
Shasta	2,747	3,612	3,478	2,100	1,650
Tuolumne	1,000	10,792	16,501	16,141	1 5,728
Trinity	2,745	7,117	9,245	3,245	6,659
Yuba	4,440	9,085	1 4,367	6,465	6,351
California	100,557	123,323	185,759	138,604	129,967

to be found in the Calaveras Mining Laws, in manuscript form, in the California State Library at Sacramento. From October 1854 to July 1857, forty-nine claims were registered by Chinese miners.   Of these, eight were listed as "located," fifteen as "bought," and the rest under the vague term of "claimed." The size of such claims depended upon the number of partners, but the average was about 150 square feet per person. This distribution of the sizes of the claims is shown in Table 7.

It is significant that 26 out of 49 claims were owned and presumably operated by two or three persons. This corroborated the contemporary observation that the rocker was still the favorite mining implement of the Chinese long after others had abandoned it.   A group of two or three persons is too small to operate anything more complicated than a rocker. If this sample is typical, the large Chinese camps that dominated the scene in 1852 either had been broken up by 1854, or had become simply residential units instead of production units.

If either of these interpretations is correct, it tends to confirm the statement of the Chinese representative before the

TABLE 7

CHINESE MINING CLAIMS IN CALAVERAS COUNTY, 1854-1857

Number of Persons Jointly Owning One Claim	Number of such claims
2	13
3	13
4	7
5	2
6	4
7	1
8	2
10	1
12	2
15	2

Committee on Mines and Mining Interests. He stated that the attempt to bring contract labor to California had proved unprofitable and had been discontinued, that most of the Chinese in the state came with their own means or those of their relatives.[50] In other words, other enterprises, notably trade, were much safer investments. Thus the amount of money invested by Chinese in commerce was estimated at $2,000,000 in 1852.[51]

One of the reasons for the apparent backwardness of the Chinese in mining methods and organization was discrimination itself. They were forced to remain relatively mobile since flight from a given community was often the most effective way of avoiding trouble. The division of interests between merchants and miners, between mining and water companies and independent miners restricted anti-Chinese riots to an essentially local incidence. For example, from Borthwick's report of dams being built in 1850 by a group of 150 Chinese miners,[52] we know that the Chinese were capable of larger undertakings and organization. The long tom, sluice, and flume were more or less permanent and immobile investments, highly conspicuous in times of prosperity and immensely vulnerable during depressions. The "portable" rocker made it possible for the Chinese to migrate from place to place to avoid persecution without abandoning their "investment." After 1858 when the white independent miners left the surface mines en masse, the Chinese independent miners ceased to be an economic or a political issue.

Part II: 1858-1867

Standardization, consolidation, and the exodus of independent miners characterized the next period of California mining. Greater uniformity in mining techniques and organization was achieved, in part through the elimination of smaller companies and independent miners. The process began late in 1858 when interest rates came down from two to two and one-half per cent per month on merchandise, and two and one-half to three per cent on commercial paper in the early part of 1858 to one and one-half per cent on collaterals.[1] This gave people who had direct access to bank credits an advantage over those who did not; small operators belonged to the latter class. The reduction in interest rates was accompanied by such efforts at modernization as the introduction of gun powder in hydraulic mining toward the end of 1858.[2]

By 1859 gun powder was extensively adopted for the purpose of shattering rocks. This process brought about a great saving of time and labor but it also materially reduced the quantity of water needed for the saturation and dissolution of gravel.[3] In the meantime, drainage problems were forcing smaller companies engaging in "hydraulicking" out of business, as tunnels had to be dug from the mines directly to rivers, by-passing the sluggish streams of high ridges.[4] This required considerable capital, which was not always available to small operators. This period of transition ended in December 1864, when heavy rainfalls in 1860-1862 and a severe and prolonged drought in 1863-1864, dealt a crushing blow to surface mining though company mining survived and recovered toward the end of that year. In 1863 alone 20,000 miners left the state to participate in only one of a series of gold rushes outside of California.[5]

Since major mining companies operated their own ditches, the fate of independent mining canal companies and that of the independent miners went hand in hand, though at the time ditch owners and miners were bitter enemies. The assessed value of the mining ditches is the most convenient, if not the most reliable index for the fluctuations or trends of surface mining. Figures in the annual report of the Surveyor-General of the state, based on county reports, were far from complete, and by no means accurate, but nevertheless indicative.[6] These figures are shown in Table 8.

TABLE 8

ASSESSED VALUE OF MINING DITCHES, 1858-1863

Counties	1858	1860	1862	1863
Amador	$ 600,000[a]	$246,300	$141,000	–
Calaveras	991,000	297,960	196,728	$157,000
El Dorado	617,970	508,870[b]	–	–
Nevada	953,700	985,800[b]	–	521,000[c]
Placer	283,106	217,600	217,600	146,600
Shasta	89,000	98,000	100,000	–
Sierra	420,650	520,950[b]	273,000	–
Tuolumne	1,481,000[a]	395,000[b]	265,000	254,282

[a]1856 figures   [b]1859 figures   [c]1865 figures

If the mining ditches of the major quartz and hydraulic companies were not included, evidence of the decline in Nevada would have been even more drastic than the figures $985,000 and $521,000 indicated. The drop from $1,481,000 to $395,700 within four years in Tuolumne county represented an extreme case since small companies dominated that area. The fact that a depression hit Shasta county before 1858 is demonstrated by these figures. The total assessed value of the ditches had been $204,400 in 1856 but had declined to a mere $89,000 in 1858. After 1863 few counties, three to be exact, continued to report on the value of the canals. After 1865 none reported.[7] By that time most of the canals in operation had become subsidiaries of the mining companies. The age of pioneer mining was definitely a thing of the past.

The most important causes for this drastic reduction in the value of the ditches were: the downward trend of costs, the resultant competition from newly constructed canals which forced a decrease in water rates and the steady decline in the yield of placer mines. The revolt of earlier miners against the high price of water had not been notably successful. By 1860, however, a substantial cut in the charge for water was achieved through a series of strikes.[8] It has been estimated that the receipts of the ditches then depreciated 10 per cent per year with no comparable decrease in operating expenses.[9] In the aftermath of these conditions and the drought of 1863-1864, few smaller companies survived.

Gold production figures are also indicative of the declining importance of placer or surface mining, the erstwhile major producer of gold. The annual gold yield in California declined from a peak of eighty million dollars in 1852 to fifty-seven million in 1856. Gold production stabilized at an annual level of forty million dollars in the years 1857 to 1860. Then the downward trend resumed. Only half as much gold was extracted in 1864 as in 1862. The heavy rainfalls in late 1864 gave mining a new lease on life and the triumph of company mining was complete. The yearly production then stabilized at a level of $17,000,000 throughout the 1860's and 1870's.[10]

By the early 1860's the majority of the surface miners were of Chinese origin. In 1860, out of the total mining population of 82,573 only 24,282 were Chinese[11]; by 1870 the corresponding figures were 30,330 and 17,363.[12] In other words, when total mining population dropped 70 per cent in ten years, that of the Chinese declined less than 30 per cent. The magnitude of this change was indeed alarming both because a large proportion of the white miners in 1870 were wage laborers, and because the exodus from "independent" mining for white miners probably terminated before 1865. Thus the mass exodus of white miners perhaps was the determining factor for the conspicuous rarity, though not complete absence, of anti-Chinese riots in the years 1859 to 1866.

The exodus of white miners three years before the Chinese is significant too. Judging from contemporary reports, gold production figures, and the assessed value of mining ditches, a mass exodus of white miners started during the 1859-1860 season and terminated five years later. The corresponding years for the Chinese were 1863-1864 and 1867. Yearly receipts of Foreign Miner's Tax again are our best index. [13] These figures are shown in Table 9. There was no downward trend during this period. In fact an upward trend among the Chinese occurred. When the exodus of white miners began, the Chinese moved in en masse and once again they served as an economic stabilizer. This entry delayed the final collapse of the mining ditches for several years. When the Chinese in turn moved out of mining, the ditches were doomed. Of course, the pattern for each county differs. Thus the number of Chinese miners in Mariposa began to drop in the 1861-1862 season. On the whole, however, 1863 was the best year for Chinese miners.

TABLE 9

FOREIGN MINER'S TAX RECEIPTS, 1859-1863

County	1859	1860	1861	1862	1863
Amador	$ 13,365	$12,748	$15,178	$14,884	$17,644
Butte	14,292	9,774	13,639	7,484	9,712
Calaveras	5,085	11,195	12,982	10,330	12,223
El Dorado	21,768	15,778	29,114	29,220	44,024
Mariposa	5,794	8,383	12,430	7,427	3,783
Nevada	2,918	3,172	3,777	3,262	4,952
Placer	11,970	13,292	18,473	24,617	22,441
Trinity	7,957	5,643	9,309	5,141	6,987
Tuolumne	8,160	8,203	5,117	4,454	7,862
Yuba	3,152	5,342	4,876	2,091	6,176
California	$119,871	$117,056	$160,778	$139,792	$186,945

Outside of Yuba and Butte counties the yearly fluctiations of the total Chinese mining population were mild. Even for those two counties the amplitudes were smaller than the 1854-1858 period. This again serves as a kind of statistical evidence for the comparative paucity of anti-Chinese riots. Riots and the expulsion of Chinese from one locality often caused inter-county migrations. However, after reaching a peak in 1863, the Chinese mining population declined drastically. It is unfortunate that we have no records for receipts of 1864 and 1867. Table 10 will furnish some idea of the magnitude.[14]

If these figures are reliable, the Chinese mining population was reduced by 68 per cent over a period of five years. The figures also indicate that the Chinese mining population in 1863 was about 60 per cent higher than the census year 1860. If we take 1863 as the base year, the decline of Chinese miners by 1868 was comparable in its amplitude to that of the white miners for the years 1860-1870 or on a general plane, in the period 1860-1865.[15]

TABLE 10

FOREIGN MINER'S TAX RECEIPTS, 1863-1868

County	1863	1865	1866	1868
Amador	$ 17,644	$ 6,852	$ 4,971	$ 1,320
Butte	9,712	7,971	10,316	4,651
Calaveras	12,223	6,957	4,472	5,383
El Dorado	44,042	19,527	14,084	-
Mariposa	3,738	2,205	3,216	1,181
Nevada	4,952	8,612	6,715	4,363
Placer	22,441	10,804	7,905	3,164
Shasta	5,077	6,752	7,806	5,863
Siskiyou	9,077	10,292	15,670	11,973
Trinity	6,987	3,331	4,707	3,532
Tuolumne	7,862	6,186	5,425	1,452
Yuba	6,176	5,425	4,246	4,592
California	$186,176	$123,067	$112,961	$60,443

The timing of the mass exit of the white miners can explain in part the dependency of the Central Pacific Railroad on Chinese laborers in the 1860's. White miners had already left the state or entered other professions while the Chinese were just beginning to make such changes.

Net immigration figures from China also corroborate this timing. These reflected a net loss in the years 1864-1867 whereas from 1860-1863, when the white miners were leaving, Chinese immigration was moderately heavy. By 1867 anti-Chinese agitation, even in the mining districts, had changed. Chinese wage earners were the new target. Though Chinese independent miners clearly outnumbered mining laborers by at least ten to one, they were more or less left alone, an interesting insight into the changing character of the California economy and society.

Part Three: 1867-1880

California gold mining during this period was noted both for stability and a high degree of concentration. The latter can best be illustrated by the fact that in some years as in 1876, forty-two leading hydraulic, drift and quartz mines produced more than half of the gold in the state, $8,357,155 out of a total of $15,610,723.[1] Its stability can be deduced from the small fluctuation in annual gold production. Contrary to the conditions in other business and in spite of the strikes of 1869-1871, disturbances of the anti-Chinese movement, and general unrest in the state, gold production was stable and actually showed a slight upturn after 1877.[2]

Though the vast majority of the Chinese at this time were still "independent" miners, they were on the whole ignored by the white miners and the press alike. They were of course no longer in serious competition with the white miners. Thus in 1870 for example, of the 30,339 total mining population, 17,363 were Chinese; of the rest 7,589 were employed by the mining companies;[3] hence there were perhaps less than 6,000 white independent miners left in the state. This was a far cry from the heyday of the Gold Rush era. Very little can be learned about the individual Chinese miners, or their white counterparts, during this period. They were forgotten men.

There were increasing incidents attendant upon the formations of Chinese mining companies in this period. It is true that around 1858, when the white miners began to leave the mines, the Chinese gradually emerged from the rocker level of mining technology. In Sacramento County, for instance, nine "mining companies" operated by the Chinese were recorded in the 1860 Manuscript Products of Industry Census. These were merely co-operatives and the number of workers was not more than five. The assessed value of the mines ranged from $1,725 to $3,600, and averaged $2,500. Wages, or per capita income of the partners amounted to $40-$50 a month compared to the $60 for other "companies" of comparable size.[4] Only in Sierra County was there evidence of Chinese miners owning a claim in excess of $5,000.[5]

The bulk of the Chinese mining companies in this period 1865-1880, employed 15-20 workers, owned a claim of two to three thousand dollars, exclusive of equipment, and engaged in hydraulic or drift mining. The Mining and Scientific Press had made passing references about such companies in Butte, Calaveras, Nevada, Placer, Sierra, Siskiyou, and Yuba counties. Unfortunately the information furnished, as a rule, is anecdotal and hence does not lend itself to a detailed analysis. In other words, there is no way of comparing their costs and profits with those of other hydraulic or drift mines.

These companies were apparently free of persecution; few incidents were recorded either in the local papers or in trade journals. Thus a Chinese mining company, incorporated in 1867, reputedly took out $800 to $1,500 per week, remained unmolested, and was still in operation in 1881. Before 1859 this would have been considered a major miracle.

The income might have been grossly exaggerated, but in a previous era such a rumor would have resulted in immediate expulsion. If these companies, and this one in particular, had been engaged in some other business, various pressures would have been brought upon them. Judging from the small investments, labor force, and wide dispersion, it can be assumed that major companies were less than eager to take over these claims, the majority of which might be marginal. The few white pioneer miners were either unwilling or unable to raise operating capital with which to plunge into hydraulic or drift mining.

During this period, while the majority of the Chinese were still independent miners, the small number of Chinese mining laborers had already become the target of persecution. When the third wave of anti-Chinese agitations in the mines broke out in 1869, it was as a by-product of struggle between labor and management. The most important factors that brought about such a conflict between miners and mine owners on the one hand, and between the white skilled laborers and the Chinese on the other, were the large scale application of "giant powder," the single-handed drill, and the discharge of a great number of Chinese trained in handling such explosives and tools by the Central Pacific Railroad. The implication of this was obvious enough; technical innovations coincided with an influx of labor supply.

From June, 1869, until August, 1871, the strike was widespread and it culminated in the so-called Sutter Creek strike. The demands of labor were the abandonment of "giant powder" as a blasting agent, a continuation of pre-1869 wage rates, equal pay for above-ground and under-ground workers, reductions in the length of working shifts, and the discharge of, and the promise not to hire Chinese workers.[7] Except on the last issue, the owners conceded nothing.[8]

The employers won the unanimous support of the press, long before the strike was settled. According to the employers, labor costs amounted to thirty to fifty per cent of the total cost; the introduction of "giant powder" and single-handed drills would reduce ten to twenty-five per cent, or an average of twenty per cent in the total cost. In one paper, for instance, the following comparison was made: with black-powder and old type drills, 60 workers, two to a drill, in an aggregate of 329 man-days, took out 188 tons of quartz and the extracting cost amounted to $5.39 per ton. With giant powder and single-handed drills, 12 workers in 174 man-days took out 106 tons, costing only $2.09 per ton, a difference of $3.20 per ton.[9] In other words, the readers were asked to believe that with new techniques the efficiency of labor increase three-fold, and costs were cut more than sixty per cent.

With these facts in hand the press charged that the Miners' League seriously retarded the development of mining in the state.[10] The trade paper urged early acceptance of equalization of wage scales between California and other states. [11] Even the experts were appalled by the unreasonable demands for equal wage without regard to skill and risk differentials.[12] Emphasis might be different, but the theme was analogous. The sooner these technological changes were confronted and accepted as a matter of fact or as an inevitable trend, the better it was for all concerned.

The formation of the Miner's League and the strikes were undoubtedly closely tied up with industrialization, unionization, and industrial disputes on a national scope. However, these issues are dealt with adequately elsewhere so we will concentrate on the local scene. The release of a large number of Cornish, Irish, and Chinese tunnel workers by the Central Pacific Railroad in April, 1869, indubitably was of grave concern to the miners. The extent of this in terms of employment is hard to determine. Records of the hiring and firing of mining laborers were a rarity. Most of the existing wage ledgers the present author has examined do not cover the critical year of 1869. Before and after the strike years of 1869-1871, there seemed to be a reasonable continuity of labor force; the notable exception being the Chinese, who were hired mostly for the construction jobs, tunnel and ditches.

The wage effect on the employment of Chinese was also indeterminate. Between 1868 and 1870 wages for underground miners had been stabilized at $3.00 per day or $90 per month; The miners were paid for actual working days in a month, usually about 26 days. [13]

Since wages fluctuated but very little around 1869 we have to carry our investigations into the late 1850's. The first mention of Chinese workers in quartz mines did not go further back than John C. Fremont's Mariposa claims. There Chinese and Cornish miners imported from England, worked shoulder to shoulder.[14] At the same time a group of Chinese was employed in handling quartz in Calaveras county.[15] One reason for the hiring of the Chinese was, to be sure, the low quality of the yield in this particular mine, a disappointing $5.00 per ton.[16] Obviously prevalent labor cost for white workers was prohibitive. Rossitor W. Raymond, commissioner of mining statistics, reported that in Merced, Mariposa, and Tuolumne Counties certain Chinese had been employed in quartz mines for ten, twelve or fifteen years before 1870.[17] If the later figure is accurate, it would push the first entry of the Chinese to around 1855.

As was pointed out before the first major reduction of wage scale for skilled workers probably came in late 1854 or early 1855. Thus the entry of the Chinese into the quartz mines was too late to have any effect. Again, judging from the rarity of agitations against Chinese mining laborers, the number of Chinese thus employed could not have been large enough to arouse antagonism. In spite of flowery rhetoric against Chinese coolies, the main target was the Chinese miner who owned a claim in the late 1850's. Moreover, the majority of the Chinese were employed in the quartz mills, where pay was lower and work tedious. One mill owner explained that the Chinese were better feeders, because they did not become impatient and dissatisfied with the monotony of labor.[18]

The second and third major wage adjustments seem to have occurred between 1865 and 1868, if the case in Mariposa was "typical." Whatever the wage scales in other counties had been, by 1869 only the mines in Sierra, Inyo, and Alpine counties maintained a slightly higher pay scale[19] than those in Mariposa. Gold production in the last two counties was negligible.

Thus, before the entry or the threat of mass entry of the Chinese into the skilled labor market on a large scale, significant wage reductions occurred. This preceded the completion of the transcontinental railroad. Thus it may be argued that the strikes prevented a drastic downward adjustment of wage scale at the critical moment by forcing the Chinese into other industries. However, since very little was known about the Cornish and Irish labor released by the Central Pacific Railroad, the effects of labor supply on wage scale are unclear.

TABLE 11

WAGE RATES FOR MINING LABORERS, [20]
MARIPOSA COUNTY, 1863-1870

Job Classification	1863-65	1866-68	1868-70
Miners	$3.50 - 4.00	$3.25 - 3.50	$ 3.00
Strikers	3.00	2.75	2.25 - 2.50
Carpenters	4.00 - 6.00	4.00 - 5.00	3.50 - 5.00
Blacksmiths	4.00 - 4.50	3.75 - 4.00	3.25 - 4.00
Machinists	4.00	4.00	3.50 - 4.00
Engineers	3.50 - 4.00	3.25	3.00 - 3.50
Firemen	2.75 - 3.00	2.75	2.50 - 2.75
Mill tenders	3.50 - 4.00	3.50	3.00 - 3.50
Mill feeders	3.25 - 3.50	3.50	3.00
Laborers	$3.50 - 4.00	$ 2.50	$2.25 - 2.50

One reason for the attack unleashed upon the Chinese was the upward trend of Chinese wages during the late 1860's and early 1870's. Judging from contemporary reports and the few wage books that are still in existence, the Chinese worked for $1.00 - 1.25 per day before 1868. After 1868 their earnings went up to $1.75 - 2.00, or even $2.30 for the skilled and $1.50 for the unskilled. [21]

Thus, relying upon his judgment of the parity of Chinese and white labor, and in consideration of the upward trend, Rossiter Raymond speculated that in time the quality of labor alone would become the sole measure of wage rates. [22] By the mid-1870's, this trend was reversed, or at least checked as the anti-Chinese movement gained new momentum. For example, in the issue of wages, the El Dorado Water and Deep Gravel Mining Company's wage ledger gave the wages of the Chinese at $1.25 for unskilled labor, $1.50 - 1.75 for skilled labor, and $50 - 60 a month for skilled miners. The same scale was maintained until 1884,[23] as the records of the Black Bear Mining Company and other mines bear out. During that time wages for the white workers fell to $2.00 to $3.00, and only first class miners could command the latter figure. [24]

In addition to the opposition from the white miners, other factors discouraged employment of Chinese, particularly the exclusive employment of the Chinese. Among the most important of these was the insistence on prompt payment of wages. The Chinese had little faith in the employer's promise to pay and would cease to work immediately if he failed to do so. As was pointed out by Rossiter Raymond, this practice was most injurious to mining enterprises in the remote districts. There cash did not always arrive on time, and the labor force could not be replaced easily. [25]

The problem was serious. Gold mining was one of the few businesses that have no receivables, as its produce was equivalent to cash. When production stopped suddenly, there could be no money to meet the payables. Therefore, to ensure regular wage payment to the Chinese workers, a large reserve of gold or cash had to be kept in the mines. This made financial control or supervision from San Francisco, where the main office was usually located, exceedingly difficult.

Whatever the attitudes of the employers toward the Chinese miners may have been, they were dependent upon the Chinese as tunnel and ditch diggers, so that a majority of the Chinese on company payrolls were construction workers. Unfortunately information on the role of Chinese ditch and tunnel workers is even more scarce. In the Manuscript Population Census there is little differentiation between those who worked on mining ditches or irrigation ditches.

It has been reported that the North Bloomfield Gravel Mining Company, one of the largest in the state, employed 800 Chinese, in addition to the 300 white workers in its ditches. [26] Records in the El Dorado Water and Deep Gravel Mining Company showed that from May 6 to the end of June, 1875, between 500 and 800 Chinese were employed at various times in a tunnel project. A total wage equal to 34,081 man-days had been paid out, at a six-day-week work schedule, averaging about 741 workers per day. The wages of the Chinese were consistently lower than those of Chinese miners. Those who handled blasting received $28.00, and those digging $26.00, while headmen received $32.50 per month. As in various construction jobs, the laborers were paid through the headmen or contractors. In contrast, those who stayed on as miners, after the project had been finished, received their pay individually and at a higher wage scale, of $32.50 to $39.00 per month. [27]

Construction works involved heavy overhead; hence wages are of special importance. Usually the accountants charged all expenses, including machinery, to the costs of the first project without bothering with depreciation. For instance, North Bloomfield imported $75,607.10 worth of tools and machinery in 1872 and were charged in toto to that construction project. Hence, for that particular job, labor cost was equal to only 55 per cent of the total cost. [28] After that labor cost was close to three-fourths of the total cost. [29] Reports from other companies using similar bookkeeping methods demonstrated the same ratio between labor cost and total cost. [30] Because of this, wages were a paramount consideration for employers in construction work. In contrast, even with the same method of calculation labor costs never went up to 44 per cent of the total cost of mining. [31]

The consideration of the cost factor explained in part the employment policies of the mining companies. In construction works, most companies hired Chinese whereas in mining the Chinese miners never constituted more than a third of the total labor force. [32] Thus the employer could hope to prevent strikes or walkouts from both the white workers and the Chinese.

The employer's preponderant concern over wage-levels was also partly influenced by high interest payments. A cursory glance at the annual reports of the mining companies would reveal the burden of interest ranging from one-fourth to nearly one-third of the total costs of labor, machinery, material, and interest combined. [33]

A question arises here in view of the high overhead and high interest charges: why did the mining companies launch such extensive construction at all? The answer is that such a project was essential to the successful operation of mines and the operating costs were small. For instance, the Blue Gravel Mining Company was in operation from 1853 to 1863.

The total gold production during this period was $315,000. But in the forty-three months after the tunnel was completed in 1864, total production reached $837,000, net profit amounted to $627,000. Operating costs were not more than $5,000 per month. [34]

   The Chinese miners were connected with the mining companies in still another way: the buying and reworking of the tailing residues. The number of Chinese engaged in this enterprise is hard to estimate. In such localities it appears that the whole Chinese population was working on tailing. [35] This illustrates the fact that the exact proportion of Chinese working in different mining enterprises is impossible to determine. The best source is the Manuscript Census. But

TABLE 12

DISTRIBUTION OF CHINESE MINERS, 1870, 1880[36]

Counties	1870		1880	
	Miners	Mining Labor	Miners	Mining Labor
Amador	1,112	10	758	1
Butte	1,167		1,605	
Calaveras	1,009	7	785	
Del Norte	171		272	
Fresno	301		153	
El Dorado	1,147		1,026	
Klamath	488	Lake	188	
Mariposa	733	24	572	
Nevada	1,373	18	1,681	
Placer	1,370	3	828	90
Plumas	695		598	
Sacramento	892		1,165	
Shasta	533		1,198	
Sierra	350	373	936	
Siskiyou	1,224	3	965	29
Trinity	909		1,392	24
Tuolumne	1,381		592	
Yuba	628	36	697	

some or most of the census takers did not take pains to differentiate.   Thus the number of Chinese mining laborers has
been under-represented. Table 12 demonstrates the problem.

According to the preceding table, the total change in the
Chinese mining population was slight. The decline in Chinese mining labor perhaps was due more to methods of record-
ing, especially in Sierra county, than to actual job mobility.
The increase in Trinity county was in part due to a partition
of Klamath county lands.

After the 1869-1871 strikes, friction between the white
and Chinese miners was reduced to a minimum at the same
time anti-Chinese agitation gained momentum along the coast.
When this anti-Chinese movement did penetrate the interior,
it retained its urban characteristics.   The Chinese were expelled from the towns but only rarely from the mines.

One of the rationales for the wage differentials between
the races was the difference in the standards of living. Opposition spokesmen maintained that the Chinese could subsist
on a few pennies a day.   However, judging from the records
of a Chinese country store in the general area of the Black
Bear mining company, Chinese laborers, many of them probably miners, paid $16 per month for board in 1874. This com-
pared to what the company boarding houses charged white
miners, $16.50 to $18.00. [37]

When the Chinese started to leave the mines between 1864
and 1868, the death knell of independent water and canal
companies was sounded. At that time some communities looked
favorably towards contracts that brought in Chinese miners to
their locale. [38] On the other hand, when company mining had
triumphed over independent mining, laborers in the mines rebelled. By this time, however, mining had ceased to be the
dominant interest in the state.   Therefore it was no longer a
major political issue. Without allies, without resources, the
strike failed. It had perhaps taught workers in other industries
a simple lesson, the need for a single dominant issue that
could unite various economic interests in the state.   The
workers in San Francisco seized upon the Chinese question.

CHAPTER III

RAILROAD AND CHINESE LABOR IN CALIFORNIA, 1862-1880

Although mining had dominated California's economy in the 1850's and early 1860's, during the late 1860's and 1870's railroads became predominant. In investment, income, and employment, however, the railroads never achieved the same pre-eminence as mining had had. Nevertheless their influence on the development of agriculture, manufacturing, and the changing economic structure of the state is of great importance. Furthermore, the railroads were not only the first "big business" in California; they were also the largest employer of wage laborers down through 1880.

Railroad construction in California was deterred by difficulties in securing risk capital and recruiting an adequate labor force. Initially, in the 1850's, capital had been attracted to mining, real estate, and trade. It was not until the value of mining ditches declined that investors looked for additional outlets for capital.

The capital needs for railroad construction have obviously always been high. This was especially true in the high-price and high-wage area of mid-nineteenth century California. Railroads in the East had been built at tremendous financial and social costs to communities which had expected prompt, extravagant, and everlasting economic gains. However, cities and towns in California were not prepared to make comparable sacrifices. For San Francisco, ocean and river transportation were considered adequate to sustain prosperity. Again, the principal product of the interior towns of California was gold, a commodity with high cash value but a low freight rate. This contrasted with the commodities of the Midwest which had a low cash value but represented bulk freight shipping. It is important to differentiate the promotional talks in the West and the genuine railroad craze elsewhere. A willingness to underwrite construction costs is the crucial test. Of course, many communities in California did raise substantial funds for the construction of railroads. The amounts, however, were commensurate neither with the capital needs of the railroads nor the wealth of the community. Hence the Central Pacific Railroad was financed, though not exclusively, by the federal government and through eastern banking firms.

Railroads in a frontier tend to have a much lower income in relation to capital investments. Investment returns were likely to be lower than in manufacturing and trade, the competitors for capital. Thus high capital requirement functioned as a deterrent to railroad development.

In addition to the difficulties in raising capital, labor constituted a problem of no lesser magnitude. While placer mining was prosperous in the 1850's wage laborers were not available in great numbers. Labor costs, therefore, were prohibitive. It was not until the mid-1860's when the Chinese had left the mines that the labor problem for railroads as well as manufacturing could be solved satisfactorily.

Short lines which had prospective heavy traffic were indeed able to commence construction in the late 1850's and early 1860's. Lines such as Sacramento Valley Railroad, which ran between Sacramento and Folsom, some 21 miles, or the San Jose Railroad which connected San Francisco and San Jose are cases in point. Little information exists about the construction stage of the Sacramento line;[1] construction laborers of the San Jose, however, were paid at $27 per month, with board. The latter constituted three meals a day, including beef, black coffee, potatoes, and fresh bread.[2] The wage scale was substantially lower than that of common laborers in the mines or in the cities.

Partly because of the problem low wages afforded, the San Jose was the first railroad to experiment with Chinese labor.[3] This event received few notices, and hardly any comments at the time, and was soon completely forgotten.[4] The fact that the early and mid-1860's was a period relatively free from anti-Chinese sentiments in part explains this lack of interest or concern. Competition between Chinese and white laborers was latent. But it was also reasonable to assume that San Jose did not employ a large enough "alien" labor force so as to attract attention or evoke protests. Again the fact that construction began in May, 1861, and the road was not open to traffic until January, 1864, suggests that a very limited labor force was employed even inclusive of the Irish and Chinese.

Though it was little known, the construction of the San Jose Railroad was a momentous event in the economic history of California. It was one of the very few major enterprises not designed primarily to serve the needs of the mines and the miners. Therefore, the foremost concern of the promoters and investors had been costs instead of completion date. A precedent for the low pay scale of construction laborers had thus been set. At the same time the linking of San Francisco and San Jose symbolized the ascendency of agriculture as a major industry and signified that San Francisco was no longer a mere appendage to the mines.

The construction of the road coincided with the decline of placer mining and the exodus of white miners. It presumably could have been completed within a shorter period of time had a larger labor force and a higher wage rate been available. However, higher wages were out of the question. As William W. Hollister generalized for railroads in California as a whole: [5]

> "I do not see how they could have been built. They might have been built, but at such an expense that they would be almost worthless. I do not see how a bushel of wheat could have been carried over the road; it would have cost more than the wheat was worth to transport it."

With the advent of bulk freight, a new set of considerations prevailed, and the precedence of cost was brought to the foreground. As world market determined the price of wheat, it indirectly set the upper limit of potential local transportation costs. Above these the farmer would be compelled to withhold the commodity from the market. This potential maximum freight rate, or the expected income of the railroad, decided its optimum capitalization, or fixed costs. These in turn formed the basis for the calculation of maximum wage rates above which capital would not be invested and the road not be built.

As long as the common laborers performed mostly odd jobs and incidental tasks, and while compensation for their labor was only a fraction of the total costs, their wage rate had been high in California. Obviously construction works could ill afford the existing pay scale. Therefore, the San Jose Railroad set a low wage rate and took whatever number of workers were available at that price.

In contrast, the position of the Central Pacific Railroad was unique because of the magnitude and the urgency of its project. The Central Pacific could not pursue the policy of a fixed low wage and a small and varying labor force. In fact, a maximum labor force was its most pressing need because of prodigious federal land grants. Whatever measures it took, the effects on the local labor market were too far-reaching to be ignored. The employment of Chinese labor was no exception. In addition, the building of a transcontinental railroad was one of the most newsworthy of items for the press.

When construction began, small sections were let out to various contractors. Before long, however, it became clear that the system of subcontracts was both inefficient and wasteful.[6] Contractors were in effect attracting workers from the same labor pool. Competition among them, more often than not, raised wage scales and interfered in operational effort. An increase in pay by one contractor lured workers from the others. They, in turn, retaliated in kind, so as to fulfill their own separate contracts. With all this hustle and bustle, the total number of laborers available for railroad construction was more or less constant. As a result, Charles Crocker & Co., and later the Contract and Finance Co., was organized to build the line east of New Castle, eliminating the waste and inefficiency of free competition. At that time some three to five hundred workers were under employment.[7]

Another problem faced by the railroad was the high rate of labor turnover. This was a legacy of the Gold Rush. Long after opportunity ceased to exist, the average workingman still aspired to be a prospector-miner—hard-working, free-spending, and above all, self-reliant and self-sufficient. Conditions changed but the ideal persisted. To many laborers signing with the railroad was but a stepping stone in a journey to the mines. At the first excitement of a gold strike, laborers abandoned construction work and rushed eastward in droves. Sometimes less than a tenth of the workers remained after a brief period of employment.[8]   Another crucial moment was payday. Many laborers got their pay, got drunk, and were never to be seen again.[9]   In brief, the quality as well as the quantity of labor left much to be desired and both problems had to be solved before construction could proceed at any speed.

   While the San Jose was built for the most part at the high tide of rising prosperity for Chinese miners, the Central Pacific Railroad began construction when recession had set in. The Chinese ex-miners were seeking employment in towns and countryside at very low wage rates. Precisely at this time the Central Pacific was plagued by various labor problems. There are indications that the occasion for the introduction of Chinese laborers had been a strike.[10]   A remark by a close associate of the management that the danger of a strike among the Chinese workers was quite remote if not unthinkable seems to corroborate this.[11]   However, the exact circumstances remain vague. The Chinese were definitely used as strike-breakers on another occasion. According to Charles Crocker's testimony to the U.S. Pacific Railway Commission, when the Irish Brotherhood of Masonry were on strike, Chinese took their places. After a few days the strike was broken.[12]

   Contradictory evidence as to whether Stanford or Crocker first suggested employment of Chinese exists, but this is not of concern to the present study. In spite of the experiment of the San Jose railroad, there was considerable doubt as to the capacity of the Chinese to perform heavy construction work.   Nevertheless fifty Chinese were hired sometime in February 1865, and Charles Crocker viewed the result with gratified astonishment.[13]   Leland Stanford commented that they were quiet, peaceful, patient, industrious, ready and apt to learn, and soon were as efficient as white workers.[14]

Within six months, between two and three thousand were employed. [15]

From all available evidence, the Central Pacific appears to have been the only employer in California to pay above the existing wage level for Chinese laborers. As late as 1867, when its labor force had almost reached its peak, agents for the railroad toured the mining counties to offer jobs to any number of Chinese at $31 per month. Their standard wage of the day for common laborers ranged between $25 and $26. [16] James H. Strobridge, chief engineer of the railroad stated at a later date, "When I was a contractor myself, I frequently had to pay them more than I liked to." [17]

According to various reports, the Central Pacific had set up labor recruiting stations in the Far East. It is reasonable to assume that the reports are true. However, the major portion of its labor force had been met by Chinese ex-miners. Between 1864 and 1867 a net loss of fifteen hundred Chinese in California was recorded. Therefore, the conclusion is inescapable that the railroad's efforts to attract new immigrants had been most ineffectual. The mass influx of Chinese occurred after the Central Pacific's labor force had already reached its maximum point.

As previously stated, the Chinese mining population reached its peak in 1863, and its ebb in 1868. During the period an estimated 10,000 Chinese left the mines. The decline in number of Chinese miners in Placer county, where the construction of the Central Pacific was under way in 1865, and in Amador and El Dorado counties which were within an 80-mile radius of the railroad reached major proportions. Since 45 per cent of the Chinese mining population resided in these three counties and the management of the Central Pacific spared no efforts in recruiting around that area, it is reasonable to assume that a majority of the four to six thousand ex-miners from the above-named counties found employment with the railroad.

Contemporary estimates of the maximum number of Chinese workers with the Central Pacific varies from 8,000 to 10,000. This point was reached between 1867 and 1868. If the number was 8,000 in the year 1867, few new immigrants could have been employed by the railroad, unless all the ex-miners re-turned to China, or worked in the San Francisco woolen and cigar factories. Even if we assume the maximum number of Chinese employed by the railroad was 10,000 in 1868, and that the figure in 1867 had been 8,000, the difference was made up entirely by newcomers. These constituted at most 35 per cent of the total labor force.

From the above evidence we may venture to conclude that the majority of the Chinese in the labor force of the Central Pacific were people who had already been in California for a number of years. They were mostly ex-miners, who had some acquaintances with English language and American work pat-terns. They were, therefore, easy to organize, train, and supervise. The railroad agents in the Orient had been less than successful in their task before 1868, and after that time had outlived their usefulness. Thus what the Central Pacific did was to absorb the majority of the unemployed or under-employed Chinese miners.

In addition to their availability and cheapness, the Chinese workers were well adjusted to "team work" as the Alta Cali-fornia commented in 1868. [18] The fact that sometimes twenty teams numbering 250 men were concentrated into a space within 250 feet caused admiration and disbelief, es-pecially among people who had experience with the disciplinary problems of white workers in early California. [19]

The wages of Chinese workers, according to Crocker, were initially set at $1 per day or $26 per month, the standard wage for Chinese at that time. These were raised to $30, and fi-nally to $35, but an exception was made for a few skilled workers. [20] The Alta California reported, "The headman also buys all provisions for the gang, pays for all, and at the end of the month receives the pay, deducts the charges, and then pays each man his balance. The men generally have from $20 to $25 each left after paying all the bills at the end of the month." [21] Judging from the $15 to $18 per month charged for food by Chinese stores in the mines, the former figure seemed to be closer to the truth. White workers received $35 and board, which cost from seventy cents to a dollar a day. [22] In other words, labor costs for white workers were 64 per cent to 90 per cent higher than for the Chinese

The idea that the concept of strikes was alien to the Chinese suffered a severe jolt on June 24, 1867. A circular printed in Chinese calling for a strike had been circulated, and on that date the Chinese laborers walked out "as one man."[23] Their demands were $40 a month—originally $45— and an eight-hour day. "Eight hours a day good for white men, all the same good for Chinamen."[24] The strike ended in complete failure within a week, according to Charles Crocker, and no increase in pay or reduction in work schedule was granted."[25] In retrospect Crocker described the strike as follows:

> This strike of the Chinese was just like Sunday all along the works. These men staid [sic] in their camps; that is they would come out and walk around, but not a word was said, nothing was done; no violence was perpetrated along the whole line. I stopped the provisions on them, stopped the butchers from butchering, and used such coercive measures.[26]

However, the statement by Crocker may be only technically accurate. The Alta California reported that previous to the strike, the Chinese were getting $31 per month, and for "reasons best known to themselves," the company officials had raised their wages to $35 per month.[27] Probably this pay increase was not entirely voluntary on the part of the company, but was intended to avert the impending strike. Thus, though the strike itself accomplished nothing, the prior threat of a walkout had achieved a pay raise of $4 per month.

Reports of the strike were widely reported if only briefly circulated in California. We know nothing about the reaction of the white workers. If newspaper comments are a fair index the public seemed indifferent. The number of Chinese on strike was put at five to seven thousand. It is hard of course to determine the accuracy of such estimates. The management wired New York, making inquiries about the feasibility of importing 10,000 Negroes,[28] so it can be assumed that the total number of Chinese was definitely above five thousand. Even the limitation raises another problem—did the remaining

Chinese refuse to strike, or did the circular fail to reach them?

One of the most persistent myths about the Central Pacific is that of the discharge of ten thousand Chinese and two thousand Irishmen when the line was completed to Ogden. There was no sudden cessation of railway construction. On the contrary, the railway boom in California commenced with the completion of the transcontinental railroad. The Central Pacific and Southern Pacific extended their tentacles throughout the valleys and mountains of the state, as the following table of railroad construction in California shows. [29]

TABLE 13

RAILROAD CONSTRUCTION IN CALIFORNIA, 1869-1878

Year	Miles
1869	339. 84
1870	105. 66
1871	122. 49
1872	218. 38
1873	51. 82
1874	101. 93
1875	152. 18
1876	398. 95
1877	157. 57
1878	159. 45

One of the immediate effects of the employment of Chinese labor by the Central Pacific was that many Chinese were trained in drilling, blasting, and other skills, which prepared them for similar jobs in mining companies. Chinese mining laborers were on the whole tolerated by their fellow workers, until 1869, i.e., when the completion of the transcontinental railroad released a large number of them on the labor market. Exclusion of Chinese mining laborers was one of the demands of the Miners' Strike, 1869-1871, as we have pointed out before.

Supplying Chinese railroad workers opened up opportunities for many Chinese storekeepers. They left cities like Marysville and Stockton in such numbers that from 1865-1868,

Chinese country stores almost disappeared from the county assessment rolls. Some came back with greatly increased capital in 1870. It is likely that some portion of the profit from supplying Chinese construction crews was invested in manufacturing of cigars, shirts, shoes, though tangible evidence is not available.

Once the Central Pacific had been constructed, a new phase of railroad construction began. It is probable that more white laborers were employed in railroad construction crews during the 1870's than had been under the Central Pacific. [30] There was an acute shortage of labor, especially on the lateral lines.[31] This is one of the reasons why anti-Chinese agitation among the railroad workers was a rarity, although three or four thousand Chinese had been working on the Southern Pacific alone. [32] Common laborers in urban centers had a strong aversion to rock-blasting and dirt-shoveling jobs. In one instance, an employer was swamped by applicants but gained only a handful of workers to his gang. "I presume five hundred, yes, a thousand, came into my office during the time I advertised in the Chronicle; they nearly worried me out; and they did not any of them want to work at the kind of work I wanted to have done."[33]

During the 1870's, there were between three and five thousand Chinese employed by various railroads in California. Of the three to five thousand released by the Central Pacific, many remained in Nevada. The Chinese population in that state jumped to 3,152 in 1870.[34] Others returned to mining in California and the number of Chinese miners there increased from 15,000 in 1868 to more than 17,000 in 1870.[35] Therefore only a small minority of the teeming Chinese population in San Francisco can be presumed to have been ex-railroad workers. From this evidence it is clear that any connection between the labor surplus existent in San Francisco and the railroads was remote. Not the railroad construction itself but the consequent general economic growth set in motion the second wave of immigration from China.

The importance of the linking of the Union Pacific and the Central Pacific in 1869 was more a symbolic one. The role of the transcontinental railroad in the increase of imports has been grossly exaggerated. Westbound railroad freight, even in the peak year of 1880, never equalled one-third of the tonnage of import by sea.[36] The full impact of the emergence of a national market was felt only after the 1873 panic, especially after a major reduction of westbound freight rates in late 1876. Eastbound traffic was operated under the existing rates to 1881,[37] when the Canadian Pacific became a competitor.

The freight reduction by itself would not have been injurious to industries in California had not a steep decline in commodity prices occurred concurrently. The growth of imports in volume from 1870 to 1880 was, on the whole, proportionate to the increase in population for that decade,[38] and the price effect of imports was much stronger than volume effect. The Central Pacific railroad had no perceptible influence on national price levels, and had been only a contributing factor in the increase in the volume of imports to California.

The Central Pacific Railroad might be only a minor factor leading to the depression of the 1870's in California, but its virtual monopoly in the state's major transportation systems, its gargantuan land grants, its incomparable economic power and political influence, and its rising revenue amidst general economic downswing, made it a fitting target of social protests.

The farm protest in the 1870's is too well known to be repeated here. It should be pointed out here, however, the Central Pacific Railroad achieved a status of virtual monopoly in California, and as a monopoly within limits, the volume of freight would remain the same regardless of rates. The railroad had everything to lose and nothing to gain by a rate reduction, since it was a price-maker and volume-taker, and its demand was inelastic. Thus it was to the advantage of the Central and Southern Pacific to set their short-haul rate, where competition was nonexistent, to the maximum level. This was especially true after 1876 following the opening up of the San Joaquin Valley. Local freight, in tonnage, was more than four times that of the through freight, as Table 14 shows.

In short, the conflict between the farmers and the railroad was direct and pervasive, while the consequence of the railroad on urban unemployment was circuitous to say the least. Furthermore, cheap Chinese labor, the main target of the labor movement, was indispensable to the farm producers in California. Therefore, a farmer-worker alliance required shrewd and determined leadership on both sides. That quality of leadership had been wanting in the 1870's, but the necessity for it was becoming evident in the changing economy of the latter half of nineteenth-century California.

TABLE 14

RAIL FREIGHTS IN CALIFORNIA, 1876-1880[39]

Year	Total Through Freight in Pounds	Total Local Freight in Pounds
1876	377, 547, 960	1, 850, 622, 680
1877	346, 478, 461	1, 751, 080, 390
1878	360, 143, 130	2, 417, 745, 600
1879	439, 368, 170	2, 541, 742, 410
1880	558, 438, 280	2, 862, 221, 310

CHAPTER IV

CHANGING ECONOMIC STRUCTURE
AND CHINESE IMMIGRATION, 1865-1880

Before plunging into a detailed discussion of the Chinese as industrial and agricultural workers, it may prove worthwhile to offer a cursory review of general economic conditions in California. Mining had dominated early California's economy insofar as it was the main field for investment and employment, while other sectors of the economy were oriented toward the needs of mining and of the miners. Because of this California constituted a distinct economic region in spite of its close trade relations with the rest of the world. The economic welfare of the state depended primarily on the production of gold. Wages rose and fell with the income and employment opportunities of individual pioneer miners. Local "manufacturing" was supplementary to, instead of in competition with, imported goods. California had its own price and wage levels, and the impact of Eastern business conditions had neither been immediate nor direct.

The dominance of gold, however, waned after the mid-1850's as a result of a reduction of gold yield, the rapid growth of especially wheat production, and the rise of manufacturing in the 1870's. This changing economic structure was a sign of maturation and coincided with the emergence of a national market. Thereafter, an increasing segment of California's economy was in direct competition with that of the East. Prices, wages, and levels of business activity began to conform with the national norm. With this development California's economy entered into a new era. The adjustments entailed by this change induced many new problems, and among them was that of Chinese labor in manufacturing industries.

The decline of the dominant position of mining in the state can be illustrated by the merchandise-treasure export ratio, and the merchandise export-import ratio (or balance of trade).

TABLE 15

CALIFORNIA'S EXTERNAL TRADE RATIO, 1848-1871[1]

Year	Merchandise-Treasure Export Ratio	Merchandise Export-Import Ratio
1848-54	1: 29	— *
1855-58	1: 13	1: 2. 1
1859-60	1: 6. 4	1: 1. 4
1860-65	1: 4	1: 0. 86
1866-68	1: 2	1: 0. 89
1868-71	1: 1. 5	1: 1. 37

*Reliable data on imports not available

Again, the rapid development of agriculture together with the concurrent growth of wheat exports was primarily responsible for the changes in California's external trade. With the development of agricultural exports, the treasure outflow was reduced vastly.   This, in conjunction with the reduction of gold production, the triumph of company mining, the advancement in banking, and the maturing local economy, brought about a reduction of interest charges.   Last, but not least, the decline of individual mining terminated the most important outlet for self-employment in early California. Thus the major deterrents to the development of industry, scarcity of capital and labor, were diminished.   Therefore, the rise of manufacturing in California came after the Civil War, after the Chinese left the mines en masse, and after the labor force of the Central Pacific Railroad had reached its maximum point in 1867.

The postwar depression touched the state only slightly. In contrast with the East, the year 1866 was one of the most prosperous in California. In spite of financial stringency in England and New York, money in San Francisco was easy, with the exception of the mid-year period.[2]

In the next year, however, there was considerable unemployment in San Francisco. As a result, there was a flurry of anti-Chinese agitation and a full round of debate as to the consequences and desirability of the employment of Chinese labor.[3] A cursory glance at those present at the Anti-Coolie Labor Meeting, March 6, 1867, will betray the fact that with the exception of the cigar makers, none of the trades were in direct competition with the Chinese. There were wine merchants, ship carpenters, plumbers, masons, boilermakers, tinners, stevadores, warehouse assistants, carriage makers, shoemakers (Chinese labor entered this field after 1867) and lumbermen.[4] In other words, the urban anti-Chinese movement from its very beginning was dominated by skilled labor and non-factory, or sweatshop workers, who were in no way competing with the Chinese labor.

The leadership and their followers in the 1867 anti-Chinese movement essentially constituted noncompetitors for the Chinese. They had no specific legislation or remedies except immigration restriction, much as the anti-Chinese agitations in the 1870's. The passage of laws discriminating against the Chinese in certain other areas of activities in no way affected job opportunities for the majority of the participants in the movement. The expulsion of the Chinese from a certain locality (as the miners did in the 1850's) would be similarly ineffective.

As in the case of 1852 there were clear divisions of interests and opinions within the state. Through persistent lobbying and agitation, the anti-Chinese forces had succeeded in persuading the Democratic party to take up Chinese exclusion as a campaign issue.[5] The movement failed to gain momentum. This can be explained in part by the fact that the number of workers who competed directly with the Chinese was relatively small. The budding sweatshop industries in San Francisco were still in their infancy. Furthermore, the recession was spotty. Shipping was reported as "uniformly active at remunerative rates; importers and jobbers enjoyed full average employment; farmers had reaped unprecedented harvests; mining was rated as fair.[6] In other words, depression was pretty much limited to certain segments in San Francisco.

The great debate of 1867 was in essence a repeat performance of the 1852 drama but with a different cast. The anti-Chinese elements, this time predominantly wage laborers instead of independent miners, argued that the Chinese depressed wages, deprived white workers of their employment, and that their customs, laws, language, religion and civilization in general were incompatible with the American way of life.[7] The governor, the Republican party, the employers, and a large number of important newspapers took the position that Chinese labor was essential, if not indispensable for the economic well-being of the state. They argued that white labor had not been displaced but on the contrary the utilization of Chinese labor resulted in a vast expansion of job opportunities for all.[8]

In 1869 California suffered a mild recession, and the divergence between levels of trade, profit, and employment heightened in 1870. A mild business downswing coincided with substantial unemployment in San Francisco. Again, the nonmanufacturing workers were at the forefront of the anti-Chinese crusade.[9]

Agricultural prosperity in California greatly mitigated the severity of the depression of 1873.[10] Farm prosperity made up a portion of the increase in exports and absorbed a large amount of imports. General business downturn commenced in 1874.

During the 1870's, California's annual merchandise export fell far short of its import, with the exception of 1875, 1878 and 1879. Initially the unfavorable balance of trade was not profound because the gold price was steady in the years 1871 to 1873 and a modest upward trend in commodity price appeared during the same period. The advance of import in 1876, however, was coincidental with a strong national downward trend in commodity prices, and a major reduction of westbound railroad freight charges.[11] For the first time in the history of California, there was an "industrial" depression.

As California kept gold as its medium of exchange throughout

the Greenback era, the consequences of the general price decline was particularly grave from October 1875 to October
1876, when commodity prices fell and gold price went up and
from October 1877 to July 1879, when commodity prices declined
at a faster rate than the price of gold.[12]   In short, the deflationary trend was even stronger in California than in the country
as a whole.

The impact of declining prices on California's manufacturing
can also be illustrated by the beginning of recessions (upper
turning points) in the major industries in regard to the size of
labor force, total value of product and the value of product
per worker.   The following table was compiled from the San
Francisco Municipal Reports and the data were collected on a
fiscal year basis (that is, 1874 means from July 1, 1874, to
June 30, 1875).

TABLE 16

UPPER TURNING POINTS OF SELECTED INDUSTRIES[13]

Industry	Size of Labor Force	Value of Product	Value of Product Per Worker
Woolen textile	1875	1874	1874
Boots and shoes	1878	1877	1874
Slippers	After 1880	1878	1876
Cigars	1879	1876*	1876**
Clothing	After 1880	After 1880	1876
Shirts	1877	1877	1876

*Total product instead of value of product
**Units of product per worker

The woolen industry in California, organized on a factory
production basis from the start and in competition on the national market, was the first to be affected.   Boot and shoe
manufacturing—partly factory, partly sweatshop in operation—
felt the recession a short time later.   Other industries did not

feel the impact of recession until 1876 or after the major price drop of October 1875 to October 1876.

In slipper and shirt manufacturing, during the 1876-1877 season, values of product per worker declined. There the total labor force and product value remained steady or actually rose. Indeed sweatshops often sought to combat price drops by increasing output. Therefore, in the fiscal years of 1876 and 1877 profit diminished as a result of stable or rising output and declining prices. As the depression deepened in 1877 and 1878, sweatshops began to cut production: the shirt industry in 1877, and the slipper industry in 1878.

In the case of slipper making, prices and profits declined first. Production cuts followed at an interval of two years, though labor still remained in the industry for another three years. In contrast, the reductions of output and labor force were concurrent in the shirt manufacturing industry. This disparity of labor mobility can be explained in part by the lack of similarities between slipper and shoe making, as the former were not made of leather.

The clothing industries included, however, various sub-branches. Hence, the trend was not as clear as in slipper or shirt manufacturing. Increase there in total product value and labor force after 1876 was due in part to an influx of shirt makers and the entry of female workers during a depression. In woolen mills, however, price drop and production cut were simultaneous and soon a sizable labor force had been laid off.

The effects of the 1875-1876 price drop were profoundly felt in California. A number of new industries had developed in the intervening years since the milder shock of 1870, and were in competition with Eastern producers on the local market. Many of the economic dislocations in California during the late 1870's were caused by Eastern competition, by the conflict between the emergence of a national market and a maturing regional economy. Had California remained predominantly a mining community in the 1870's, price drops in manufactured goods would have been most beneficial.

Moreover, the 1870's were a transitional period in numerous

industries from sweatshops to factory modes of production. High requirements for capital and managerial skills of factory production prevented the majority of sweatshop owners from entering the field. Mass-produced, low-priced products encroached on local markets which had been hitherto served by local sweatshops. California manufacturers were faced with the danger of elimination in the late 1870's. Unable to fight these economic forces, small manufacturers and laborers in California chose to wage their battle against the Chinese.

Aside from these external or inter-regional factors, California's manufacturers had serious regional problems to cope with. The effects of high interest rates and high wages have been discussed previously. It suffices to state here that if these were of great importance in the 1850's and the 1860's, they were more so in the 1870's when Eastern competition was not latent but intense, not intermittent but constant.

The scarcity of women laborers posed a serious problem for the development of various light industries in California. The preponderant male population in a mining frontier is a fact too well known to require lengthy documentation here. As late as 1880, for every female worker in manufacturing, there were eleven male workers in California. [14]

In addition to the unequal distribution of the sex ratio in its population, high per capita income in early California also kept white women and children out of the labor market. Many industries were compelled to start with Chinese labor. In the mid-1870's for the first time in the history of California, a substantial number of females and minors were seeking employment. Many complained that the Chinese barred them from employment.

Large scale substitution of females for Chinese labor in jobs usually held by women in other states was not entirely feasible in California in the late 1870's. There simply were not enough of them. The fact that they sought employment in a glutted labor market caused their number to be greatly exaggerated by casual observers. Secondly, they were entirely inexperienced. According to John S. Hittell, a certain shop giving work to all skilled female applicants could obtain only twenty female sewing-machine operators. [15] Moreover, it took them entirely too long to acquire a new skill. For instance, in shirt making, the females needed one to two years to finish their apprenticeship in contrast with six to eight months for the Chinese. [16] According to the same source, even when the girls were paid at a higher rate on piece work they failed to make anything near the same wage as the Chinese. [17]

Moreover, boys and girls (in California any member of the fair sex was a girl) were subjected to discipline with great difficulty. As one employer related his experience: [18]

> I never could rely upon them performing their work satisfactorily. If I would leave the factory and go up the street, when I came back I would find them throwing matches all over the factory, the floor covered with them, and they would be burnt up; and sometimes I would find them on the top of the two story building chasing each other all over the roof. By such things they destroyed a great deal of property, and I found I could not control them at all.
>
> The next change I made was to try girls in the packing of matches and putting them up, and I found more difficulty with them than I did with the boys, and I could not do anything with them.
>
> It was utterly impossible to set them to work and give them instructions that they would abide by. They would make little changes today, little changes tomorrow, and in a week you would find them doing entirely different work from the instructions you gave them.

As for the Chinese he stated: [19]

> You take a Chinaman, a green China boy, into your factory and show him just how to do a thing, and if you leave him and come back, if it is a year afterward, you find him doing the work precisely as you instructed him.

He attributed the disciplinary problems to high income of the California worker. [20]

> I think it is more the force of habit, their custom of living, the parents not having to depend on the labor of children to contribute to the family support. I think,

probably it would be a proper instruction to place upon
it to say that the laboring class here, as a general
thing, depended upon the labor of the head of the family for the family support, and that they do not depend
upon the labor of their children. I think that is the
cause.

From the late 1860's, as gold yield declined and manufacturing developed, cost-price spread became the primary concern. California's wage structure, therefore, is another key
issue. As we have mentioned before, the general wage level
in California rose and fell with the income and employment
possibilities of independent miners, but the degree of Eastern
contact or competition, direct and indirect, exercised a strong
influence in determining the wage level of specific trades.
Seamen's pay is a case in point. The income level of the
miners set the minimum below which the crew members refused
to work, and price differentials between East and West, or
freight charges or profitability, determined the maximum level
that the shipper would be willing to pay. It would not be difficult to recruit seamen in the East at $15 a month, but as
soon as the ship docked at San Francisco, their pay had to be
raised to $80, $100, $150 or even $250 to avoid desertion, or
to recruit new members.[21] As general price levels began to
decline in California during the mid-1850's, price differences
between Eastern states and the Pacific coast were reduced.
Seamen's pay on clipper ships was the first to approach the national average of $20 per month in San Francisco.[22]
The year 1853 had been the first year in which anything
resembling a standard wage rate in California came into existence. The following is a table of remunerations on various
trades before and after a series of strikes in July and August,
1853.
The differences in pay between the bricklayers and carpenters, on the one hand, and shoemakers and tailors on the other,
were astounding indeed. There seems to be no evidence of a
dire shortage of the former, or a glut of the latter. Among the
predominantly male population of a mining frontier, tailoring
was not likely to be done at home. Furthermore, after the

TABLE 17
WAGE RATES IN 1853[23]

Trades	Wage Rate Before Strike (Per Day)	Wage Rate After Strike (Per Day)
Bricklayers	$8-10	$10
Stone cutters, plasterers*	8	10
Carpenters, joiners	7	10
Printers	7	10
Tinners	4-8	7
Shoemakers,** tailors	4	4
Common laborers	4	4

*Plasterers got only $9 per day.

**Or $100 per month without board.

strike most trades were able to obtain substantial wage increases; tailors and shoemakers were notable exceptions. The strength of "unions" appears irrelevant in this case. What really depressed the wage of the latter group was the volume and the price of imports. Commodity prices set the upper limit of wage level. For those trades whose services could not be performed in the East and then transported to the Pacific coast, the remuneration for labor was on the whole high. Conversely, heavy imports coincided with low wage rates.

If this had been the case in the 1850's, it was all the more true in the 1870's. Degree of Eastern competition in great part explains employment and wage patterns in the shoe, cigar and clothing industries. Chinese labor in these trades was the consequence of low price and low wage. It was not the cause, hence their expulsion would have been a very ineffective means to raise wages, or even employment.

The low pay of the common, unskilled laborers in the late 1860's and afterwards was a major cause of labor unrest. In the short run, workers were embittered for having been denied what they considered as a living wage. In the long run, labor mobility was hampered. Wage differentials between the skilled and unskilled kept workers in their own trade even when opportunities in other fields seemed better. This is not to infer that there would be perfect labor mobility otherwise, but to point up a person's reluctance to leave a $3.50 or $4.50 job for a $1.00 or $1.50 while learning a new skill.

As long as common laborers were primarily employed in odd jobs, and their wages constituted only a fraction of the total costs, pay was relatively high. But the labor intensive industries, such as construction work and numerous sweatshop industries, could not operate at that wage level. Thus, large scale levees were seldom contemplated in early California though many towns and much farmland were repeatedly flooded.[24] Again, costly as it might be to ship machinery to the mines, road building was a rather late development. Scarcity of capital and labor was an important factor. It was no hindrance, however, to the construction of mining canals. Anticipated returns on investments were the real deterrents. In the fabulous era of the mines, cost or wage was no concern, but that day was soon over. It was not until the displaced Chinese miners joined the ranks of the pick and shovel brigade that the construction boom in irrigation, reclamation levees, railroads, and harbor improvements actually started. Not until the Chinese were available in great numbers were various manufacturing industries established and orchards extensively cultivated.

The presence and the availability of a large Chinese labor force had, in a few instances, "prevented" strikes on the part of white workers from being successful. However, the overall effect on wage levels was probably negligible. Low wage rates had been established, in most cases, before the entry of the Chinese. Moreover, many of the strikes were for an increase in wages; such demands rarely were successful except during a period of expansion.

It is next to impossible to discover and to interpret the effects of Chinese labor on the employment of white workers in construction and related fields. With only scattered information on the financial condition of such projects, it would be imprudent to venture an opinion as to the employer's ability or willingness to pay the wage differentials between the Chinese and white laborers—$30 to $32.50 for the former, and $30 to $35 with board for the latter.[25] Some credibility must be given to the employer's claim that had it not been for the Chinese, many projects would not have been started.

Remuneration of labor on a racial basis had been the custom in Southern California; such differential discrimination was only latent in the North until the 1860's when an increasing number of Chinese left the mines in search of other employment. By the mid-1860's, a standard rate of $1 per day had been established except for those with special skills.[26] Because of this uniform pay, there was a greater mobility among the Chinese workers. A transfer of jobs entailed little or no reduction in pay.

As might have been suspected, the flow of immigrants from China reflected job opportunities for the Chinese in California. To a point, the employers' assertion that the demand for labor regulated the volume of immigration contains a certain element of truth.[27]

In general, Chinese immigration until 1880 can be divided into four periods. These in turn reflect the circumstances in California. From 1850 to 1863 mining afforded the Chinese fair opportunity. In spite of riots and persecutions, these years saw the first wave of heavy immigration. From 1864 to 1867, as the placer mines were giving out, more Chinese left California than immigrated there. From 1868 to 1876 the agricultural, manufacturing and construction boom touched off another wave of immigration. From 1877 to 1880, as the depression deepened, departures nearly counterbalanced new arrivals.

From 1852 to 1863 the fluctuations of annual Chinese immigration corresponded closely to the opportunities in mining, and the intensities of anti-Chinese sentiments. Until 1852, Chinese immigration was insignificant, and most of the immigrants stayed in the cities. In the golden years of surface mining, 1852 and 1854, net immigration figures reached the all time peak of 18,258 and 13,754 respectively.[28] Reactions on the part of white miners were both immediate and violent, and in the following years, 1853 and 1855, departures exceeded arrivals. Population flow across the Pacific resumed immediately, though at more moderate rates, as the yield of surface mines declined. According to the San Francisco Custom House, figures for the eight years, 1856-1863, there was a net gain of 28,357 Chinese immigrants in California, [29] which was less than 90 per cent of the two-year total for 1852 and 1854. Judging from the receipts of the Foreign Miner's Tax, the low point of Chinese in mining came at some time just before 1860, when not more than 70 per cent of the Chinese were engaged in mines. At the peak year, 1863, the figure rose to 80 per cent or 85 per cent. [30]

For the years 1864-1867 departures surpassed arrivals from China in spite of employment opportunities in railroad and manufacturing. These were the twilight years of individual mining. During this period, about 10,000 Chinese left the mines. Nevertheless, at the end of 1867, 45 per cent to 50 per cent of the Chinese were still miners. About 8,000 or 21 per cent were employed by the railroad, and about 1,200 to 1,400 in the cigar, shoe and woolen manufacturing industries. [31] It was also during this period that an increasing number of Chinese found employment as domestic servants and launderers. Unfortunately precise information is not available. A few Chinese had left for the mountain states in search of gold. However, the trend toward wage labor was unmistakable.

From 1868 to 1876 Chinese immigration reached a new peak. During this period, it was the budding manufacturing industries in San Francisco, hop and fruit raising in Santa Clara County, truck gardening in and around San Francisco, Sacramento and lesser cities, levee, irrigation and reclamation projects, and later fruit raising and harvesting in the San Joaquin Valley, that attracted and absorbed the new immigrants from China. By 1876, manufacturing industries employed most of the Chinese—about 14,000 in San Francisco and more than 15,000 in the state as a whole. The Chinese mining population continued to decline during this period.

By 1876 less than 12, 500 remained. Construction and agricultural laborers, including those employed by the railroads,
were no less numerous than the miners. Seven thousand were
employed as servants, and five thousand in laundries.[32]

As the recession set in, an anti-Chinese movement spread
and immigration waned. At the same time Chinese were leaving California in increasing numbers for other states and territories, especially Washington, Nevada, Arizona, Wyoming,
Oregon, New York, Colorado and Louisiana. In 1870, there
were only 13, 972 Chinese in the United States residing

TABLE 18

MAJOR OCCUPATIONS OF CHINESE IN 1880

Occupation	Number	Percentage of the State Total
Agricultural and harvest laborers	3, 380	14. 2
Gardeners and garden laborers	2, 146	48
Farmers and tenants	1, 590	-
Domestic servants	7, 918	34
Hotel, restaurant keepers and helpers	630	10
Common laborers	11, 710	20
Launderers	5, 435	79. 6
Peddlers	1, 287	-
Boot and shoe makers	2, 359	52
Brick makers	316	44
Cigar makers	2, 717	84. 4
Woolen mill operators	254	32. 7
Clothing factory laborers	644	
Tailors and sewing machine operators	885	-
Miners	10, 024	27
Fishermen	1, 193	39

outside of California; a decade later this figure reached 30,333. [33]

In spite of anti-Chinese agitation and under-employment in the late 1870's, Chinese in the manufacturing industries still remained in their respective trades. The trend toward service industries remained at an initial stage. Table 18 shows the major occupations of Chinese in 1880. [34]

CHAPTER V

AGRICULTURE, 1850-1880

Part I: General Background

One of the characteristics of agriculture in nineteenth-century California was its conspicuous lack of subsistence farming. Agriculture was oriented from its infancy toward the market provided by the miners, cities, and towns. The salient features of commercial agriculture were, perhaps, made more prominent by the spectacular growth of the economy. Credit, price, transportation and labor played much more important roles than in other frontier regions. California's farming was a business enterprise almost from the very beginning.

Much of the land in California, of course, had been disposed of during the Spanish and Mexican eras in large grants. Few of the landholders were willing to part with their lands in small lots except at "exorbitant" prices. Initial investments in land for small farmers, therefore, were larger than in other frontiers. Moreover, uncertainties in land titles often led to the exhaustion of the financial means of the contesting claimants in long litigations.[1] Such situations imposed additional hazards on farm credit and increased its charges.

The high original investment for farms in California can be illustrated by the ratio between the amount of the improved farmland and the value of farms in 1850 and the differential percentage increases of the two between 1850 and 1880. Both factors are indicative of the high price of unimproved land in California. This initial high cost of farmstead in relation to the improved acreage and the drastic reduction of this ratio

67

afterwards are characteristic of a frontier region, but the slow
increment of the land value in California in the years 1860
to 1880 suggests the entry price in 1850 was excessive, as
the following table indicates.[2]

TABLE 19

IMPROVED ACREAGE AND FARM VALUATION RATIO, 1850-1880

State	1850	1860	1870	1880
California	$120	$20	$22.7	$24.6
Pennsylvania	47	66	94	106
Wisconsin	28	35	50	68

The initial high fixed cost of farms, the consequent low returns in additional investments, can also be seen in the
following table.[3]

TABLE 20

PERCENTAGE INCREASES OF IMPROVED LAND
AND LAND PRICE IN CALIFORNIA, 1850-1880

	1850-1860	1860-1870	1870-1880
Improved land	7,500	150	72
Value of farms	1,250	50	27

The legacy of Spanish and Mexican land grants is also illustrated in the size of farms in California. As a rule, with
an increase in the number of farms in an area, a concurrent
reduction in the size of farmsteads occurs. This holds true
for the frontier state of Nebraska as well. Wisconsin and
California represent departures from the normal trend of decreasing size of farms. The average unit size of farmstead
in Wisconsin was somewhat below the national average, however, while that of California was several times larger. Thus

TABLE 21

COMPARISONS OF THE NUMBERS AND SIZES OF FARMS, 1860-1880[4]

State	Total Number of Farms			Average Size of Farms (Acres)		
	1860	1870	1880	'60	'70	'80
California	18,716	23,724	35,934	466	482	462
Nebraska	2,789	12,301	65,387	226	169	157
Pennsylvania	156,357	174,041	213,542	109	103	93
Wisconsin	69,270	102,904	134,332	114	114	114
United States	2,044,077	2,659,985	4,008,907	199	153	134

in California an increase in the number of farms was not accompanied by an influx of small farmers as in other states. In short, capital requirements for agriculture remained high in California to 1880. Entry was by no means easy.

This being the case, it was not surprising to find the conflicts between the farmers and the railroad, between large and small farm producers, or the split between the large and small farmers over the Chinese issue in the 1870's. The relevancy of high fixed cost in farming to the unity within the farm movement and the stability of the farm-labor alliance in California cannot be minimized.

One consequence of these large farms was the high proportionate requirement of hired labor (though the extent of labor needed on larger farms has often been exaggerated). Except during the Gold Rush days, farm prices in California were determined not by local supply and demand but by world market conditions. As a consequence, commodity price set the upper limit of both profit and wages. Therefore, the level of wages and the labor supply available at these wages were controlling factors alike in the volume of farm production and the profit margin. Thus the agricultural developments in California and the supply of Chinese labor were intricately related.

Again, the high proportion of labor cost can be demonstrated in the ratio of labor expenditure to the total farm income. The figures of 1870 illustrate this. In that year, wages for agricultural labor in California were approaching the national level, and the shift from wheat to fruit culture had not yet taken place. Neither California's wage level, nor its labor input per acre was materially above the national average, but its labor expenditure was extremely high.[5]

TABLE 22

LABOR EXPENDITURE-FARM INCOME RATIO, 1870

State	Ratio
California	1: 4. 8
Mississippi	1: 7
Pennsylvania	1: 8
Wisconsin	1: 9. 6
Nebraska	1: 9. 8

Farmers in California suffered from the usual hindrances of unequal tax burdens, uncertain access to credit and high borrowing charges, high seasonal fluctuation of prices, expensive marketing costs. The cycles of boom and bust in California seemed to be of larger magnitude and higher frequency than many regions in the United States. The earlier cycles of potatoes, barley and wheat in 1852-1854,[6] and that of fruits in 1873-1878,[7] are cases in point.

The protests of the grain producers against the exploitation by middlemen were too well known to require repetition here. The bargaining position of the fruit producers in California before 1880 was vastly weakened by the lack of durability of their products. Vineyardists in the Los Angeles area were compelled to sell their crops to a particular buyer because of market agreements between some large wine makers.[8] Only such giant grape producers as Henry Douglas Bacon, with ready access to bank credit, and a determination to enter even into the manufacturing of wine if necessary, could break that collusion.[9]

In short, agriculturists in California were handicapped by high capital requirements and operating costs, harassed by inadequate credit and high interests. They were tormented by declining world prices, exorbitant freight rates, and high marketing costs and looked upon the Chinese as a godsend. Chinese laborers, available after the mid-1860's at constant cost since an increase in demand had little or no effect in wage rates, were readily praised. They were recognized for "patient docility and remarkable facility of imitation," (i.e., ability to acquire a new skill at a relatively short span of time), "mechanical exactitude and singular carefulness in performing their tasks," "constant industry" having "no wasteful habit" and the fact that they gave board to themselves.[10] In other words, they were dependable and cheap.

The development of agriculture and its employment of Chinese labor was closely connected with irrigation and reclamation. The earliest successful irrigation projects outside Los Angeles were in Yolo county; they were of relatively small dimensions and on the most favorable location.[11] In other areas agriculture went beyond the experimental stage only in the late 1860's. The San Joaquin Valley, for instance, is typical. There W. F. and Joseph Montgomery and their associates took out a patent of 500,000 acres of swamp land in 1857. Small canals and ditches were constructed through Tulare county in 1859-1865, from the Kern River. Development was far from rapid and the land changed hands several times while difficulties arose in raising capital to fulfill reclamation requirements of the original patent.[12]

An irrigation project could never be an attractive investment prospect during the days of the mining canal boom. After the failure of the canals in the early 1860's, however, irrigation construction was further delayed for lack of labor. Displaced miners made very poor construction laborers, and as late as 1863, the Kern River project had to depend on Mexican and Indian labor.[13]

Though a number of irrigation projects had begun construction earlier, only after 1868 did capital investment in irrigation and reclamation reach a high water mark. The capitalization of the Tide Land Reclamation Company at $12,000,000, and the San Joaquin and Kings River Canal and Irrigation Company at $10, 000, 000, [14] compared favorably with that of the major mining companies and surpassed even the largest manufacturing concerns.

Construction works, of course, were high cost industries; wages were the primary concern of the prospective investors. The dependence of such projects on cheap Chinese labor can hardly be exaggerated. It was no mere coincidence that most of the irrigation and reclamation companies were formed after 1865 when thousands of Chinese left the mines or were released by the railroads seeking employment elsewhere.

The number of Chinese working on one single project sometimes reached 3, 000 or 4, 000. [15] Men were usually hired through a contractor, and each earned about a dollar a day. [16] On some occasions they were paid by piece work at ten cents per cubic yard of earth dug. [17] This was a considerable saving from the 30 cents per cubic yard estimated by the commissioner's report. [18] The major portion of the saving perhaps came from wage differentials. The common wage for white workers was $35 per month plus board, and for the Chinese $25 to $30, [19] although they provided their own board.

The Manuscript Population Census gives but a very imperfect survey of Chinese construction gangs. The 1870 Manuscript Population Census, for example, listed 669 irrigation and reclamation workers in four counties while in 1880 the figure was reduced to less than 200. [20] The latter figure is understandable as irrigation canal construction was at a low ebb in 1880, but the former should have been much larger. At the peak of construction, in the activity around 1874 and 1875, Chinese laborers in irrigation, reclamation and levee works must have numbered to five or six thousand. Unfortunately we have no material to corroborate this.

Part II: Farming, 1850-1880

Since the focus of attention in California was on Chinese miners in the 1850's and on Chinese urban workers in the 1870's, information on Chinese in farming is extremely

sketchy. During the early days the Chinese followed closely
the pattern of occupational shift of the Latin Americans. The
latter took up potato farming and truck gardening after having
been expelled from the mines. The Chinese entered into
farming in the late 1850's, and those recorded as farmers in
census reports practiced potato and market gardening at the
same time.

In 1860 the typical Chinese-owned farm was usually operated by a single person, and the total assets for each did
not exceed $650.[1]   In 1870, the average size of the farms
became somewhat larger, and the total annual income of each
unit ranged from $800 to $3,000. One-third of the income of
the average farm came from market gardening.[2] Ah Yet, in
Sacramento, derived $8,000 of its total $9,500 from orchards.[3]
In 1880, if San Joaquin county were typical, the majority of
the Chinese farmers paid their rent in crops. Their labor cost
was from $500 to $2,000 per year. A farmer averaged 200
bushels of potatoes per acre and planted one-third of his land
in peas or other garden products.[4] Many of them paid $25 to
$30 a year an acre as rent.[5] Their distribution was, of course,
uneven, as Table 23 illustrates.[6]

Table 23 indicates that the Chinese entered into farming
in large numbers only during the 1870's. The 1880 figures
include farm laborers who worked on the farms operated by
Chinese. In some counties there are difficulties in disentan-
gling the two. Moreover, many of these farms were owned
and operated on a partnership basis. Thus, in Sacramento
county, out of the 64 farms in 1880, only 16 were owned by
a single individual. The proportion in San Joaquin County,
18 out of 32 was somewhat larger, while the three largest
single-owner farms in Sacramento hired 11 laborers each.

Alameda County had the largest concentration of single-
owner farms—14 out of 24—and 8 out of the 24 farms employed
more than 10 laborers each. On the other extreme, one farm
in Union township, San Joaquin County, had 13 partners, but
employed only two workers.[7]

From the sizes of the Chinese farms and their annual incomes, it probably can be assumed that these farms did not
compete with the neighboring wheat farmers. The productivity

TABLE 23

DISTRIBUTION OF CHINESE FARMERS, 1860-1880

	Year		
	1860	1870	1880
Alameda			244
Butte			28
Colusa			31
Constra, Costa			162
El Dorado	2		
Kern		3	18
Mariposa	2		
Mendocino			6
Merced			13
Monterey			4
Napa			65
Nevada		1	1
Sacramento	3	37	558
San Joaquin			276
San Mateo			9
Tuolumne		4	
Yolo	1	7	19
Total	8	52	1, 434

of the Chinese farms, per acre and per worker, compared favorably with those operated by the white tenants as recorded
in the agricultural census. However, detailed analysis is
handicapped by the difficulties in correlating the information
from the population and the agricultural census. The former
gives only the number of the workers residing on a certain
farm during the census-taking period, while the latter gives
only the total labor cost per year. No means exists by which
the exact nature of the seasonal demand for labor, nor the actual annual earnings of a farm laborer can be discerned. In
the case of the Chinese, there is an additional difficulty: the
population census shows only the names of the owners, while

elsewhere the name of the farm or the co-operative was usually
recorded.

If the number of the Chinese farmers was rather negligible,
that of the Chinese gardeners was enormous by comparison.
Market gardens as a rule were located near the population
centers. During or before 1860 Chinese gardeners were concentrated in San Francisco and the mining counties. By 1870,
because of a population shift, the number of Chinese market
gardeners showed a drastic reduction in such mining counties
as El Dorado, Sierra, and Tuolumne, while registering a spectacular increase in Santa Clara, Tehema, and Alameda counties. The shift toward the coastal area continued through the
1870's, and, following the railroad, Chinese gardeners invaded Southern California in the 1870's. A tabulation of this
distribution follows. As a rule the size of the gardens was
fairly small. Their total annual income hardly ever exceeded
$4,000 according to the U.S. Manuscript Agricultural Census.
In the county assessment rolls in Sacramento, San Joaquin,
Los Angeles and Yuba counties, the overwhelming majority of
the Chinese gardeners were assessed at a value of $500 or
less. Only the exceptional property valuation came up to
$1,000. Of those Chinese who reported personal property of
over $1,000, few were gardeners by profession—one in 1860,
and four in 1870.[9]

The number of persons working on each garden was also invariably small. In some counties as San Joaquin and Santa
Clara, the largest labor force in both 1870 and 1880 numbered
nine. Tehema County presented a unique case, however. In
1870 in that county there were 9 market gardens operated by
Chinese, 4 of which had a total of 12 partners, averaging 3
per unit. Of the remaining 5, each headed by a single person,
one employed 14 laborers, another 23, and the other three,
39 workers each.[10] In 1880, however, the number of gardens
increased to 31. Eighteen of these had less than 8 workers
each while the largest employed 18 laborers.[11] This seems
to indicate the breaking up of large truck gardens occurred in
the 1870's.

San Francisco was another place where it is even difficult
to determine the size of the productive units. For instance,

TABLE 24
DISTRIBUTION OF CHINESE GARDENERS

County	1860	1870	1880
Alameda	8	109	72
Amador	12		15
Butte	11	43	81
Calaveras	26	24	2
Colusa		1	28
El Dorado	30	16	26
Kern			12
Los Angeles		16	216
Marin	2	2	12
Mariposa	15	5	3
Merced	3	3	11
Mono			7
Napa			19
Nevada	15	51	79
Placer	39	66	64
Plumas		4	4
Sacramento	120	72	184
San Diego		8	13
San Francisco	34	117	135
San Joaquin			75
San Luis Obispo			7
Santa Clara		87	38
Shasta	4	18	66
Sierra	31	3	1
Siskiyou		2	14
Solano		1	47
Sonoma			12
Stanislaus	8	16	9
Sutter		12	82
Tehema		171	190
Trinity	5	12	6
Tulare		6	64
Tuolumne	42	2	10
Yulo	4	22	47
Yuba	44	68	87
CALIFORNIA	472	668	1,783

there were occasions of some twenty or thirty gardeners living
in one house though it would be erroneous to conclude that
they worked on the same garden plot.   Starting in the late
1860's there was a division of labor in the production and
distribution of vegetables in San Francisco.   In 1870 there
were 78 Chinese clearly identified as vegetable peddlers in
the Manuscript Population Census; for some reason there were
only 90 in 1880. Of the 776 peddlers reported in that census,
at least 300 were probably vegetable peddlers.[12]   However,
for our purpose, it makes little difference as the vast majority
of them bought their goods from wholesale stores downtown,
thereby distributing the products of white market gardens.

On the whole the Chinese were good gardeners in the sense
that their produce looked "large and fair as well as crisp and
succulent." In addition, their products were cheap.   But most
important they were brought to the door steps of the prospective buyers.[13]   Outside of San Francisco this function was
performed by the producers, the gardener, or his employee.
This accounts for the somewhat larger working force per unit
in larger cities such as Sacramento and Los Angeles.

As far as Chinese orchardists are concerned, the information available leaves much to be desired.   In the Manuscript
Population Census, outside of Santa Clara County, the group was
classified as farmers or gardeners even though the major share
of income came from fruits. The Manuscript Agricultural Census
for this period is very incomplete.   In the year 1870 in Santa
Clara County there were 174 Chinese cultivating strawberries,
23 cultivating berries, and 7 cultivating hops.   These were
obviously small producers since the largest unit employed a
labor force of 10.[14]

General descriptions of the Chinese orchardists in the
newspapers furnished seemingly only half truths. According
to one report, the Chinese rented ranches from the large land-
owners, employed 15 to 20 men, and paid $10 to $16 per
month plus board, as compared to the usual wage of $22.50
to $25.00 with board which the white employers were paying.
The Chinese orchardists themselves were said to live like
kings.[15]

If this was true, it must have been exceptional. Through-out the 1870's, in San Joaquin and Sacramento counties, most of the orchards were assessed at a value for less than $800 each in the county assessment rolls. Only four, all in Sacramento county, had a valuation of over $1,000. These were evaluated in 1878 at $8,655, $6,000, $4,205, and $3,654 respectively.[16] These large orchards were perhaps owned by several storekeepers on a partnership basis. In order to diversify their holdings, Chinese storekeepers often went into partnership, investing in farming or orchards.

Most of the Chinese who leased land for short terms were but sharecroppers. Aside from attending the gardens or orchards, they stored and cut hay, drained water, made boxes or baskets for fruits, and performed numerous other services and duties in the house or on the farm. Most of these chores were ones which white tenants refused to perform. In other words, by "renting" land to the Chinese, the agriculturists minimized the labor requirements on their own farms or ranches. The Chinese "tenants" received one-half of the proceeds of the vegetables and two-fifths of the fruits, whereas the white tenants usually demanded one-half of both.[17]

In all, Chinese farmers, gardeners, and orchardists formed only an insignificant part of the farming population. In 1860 there were only eight Chinese among 20,826 farmers and planters in the state who cultivated a small plot of land and employed no laborers.[18] In 1870 there were 346 out of 24,061, and in 1880, 1,434 out of 43,489.[19] These figures for the Chinese include both Chinese operators and laborers working for them; those for the state include operators only.

The number of Chinese gardeners and Chinese laborers under their employ constituted from less than one-fourth of the total in 1860 and 1870 with 472 out of 1,800 and 668 out of 2,648 respectively to slightly less than one-third in 1880 with 1,738 out of 4,390.[20] However, these two sets of figures are not strictly comparable. Those for the state as a whole included only owner-operators while those for the Chinese included both gardeners and garden laborers. Moreover, the figures for the Chinese are necessarily larger because many of them were part-time vegetable vendors. Judging from this, about three times as many Chinese vegetable peddlers in 1880 were distributing produce bought from San Francisco wholesale stores; they were not merely retailing the products of the Chinese gardens in that city. The Chinese could not have controlled more than one-fifth of the market for vegetables even in 1880, even though they were repeatedly charged with monopolizing the market. [21]

Part III: Agricultural Laborers, 1860-1880

One of the most serious problems in agriculture during this period was the procurement of an adequate and dependable labor supply. Fluctuations in labor requirements at various stages of production made the situation even more troublesome. A favorable example of the contemporary farm producers' was the variable demand for labor on a 1,200-acre beet farm. About 300 workers were needed for a single week of hoeing. Then, for an interval of three weeks their services would not be required until the second hoeing when 300 laborers were again employed. This was followed by a second lay-off until the third hoeing.[1] Under such circumstances, both availability and abundance of temporary laborers were essential to the operation.

A detailed analysis of seasonal labor requirements in nineteenth-century California is rendered next to impossible by a paucity of information. A current study is quoted here to illustrate the magnitude of fluctuations of labor demand for San Joaquin Valley.

TABLE 25

SEASONAL LABOR REQUIREMENTS IN SAN JOAQUIN[2]

	March 15	October 15
Total labor force	118,000	257,000
Temporary laborers	25,500	159,000
Percentage of temporary laborers	21%	61%

The extraordinary absolute and percentage increases of the temporary labor force from March to October are indicative of the pressing problem of labor supply even though seasonal fluctuation in the 1870's would hardly be as great as that of the twentieth century.

Because the vast majority of the farmers in the United States were grain producers, their concept of labor requirements dominated the thinking of the nation for centuries. Cotton farming, with its characteristics of high labor demand was considered as a peculiar institution of the South. The idealized and romanticized family farm myth was transplanted to California lock, stock and barrel. One of the most persistent and pervasive components of this myth was that by keeping the farms small, the need for farm laborers could be kept at a minimum. Thus class differences were obliterated, and social mobility facilitated. Whatever amount of truth the image might have contained in grain-producing areas, its applicability to fruit-raising regions was extremely tenuous. Again analogy serves, according to a current study of a total of 5,860 man hours required to operate a twenty-acre peach orchard with a ten-ton yield, 3,810 man hours or 65 per cent of the requirement must be hired labor.[3] Labor requirements of small farms fail to conform to the public image.

In California the development of fruit culture was delayed by the scarcity of labor no less than the inadequacies of credit and transportation facilities. In the 1850's hiring labor in Southern California—the grape producing area—was characterized by individual contract. Every laborer bargained for his own worth, and employers had to be familiar with the ability and dependability of each and every worker.

By the years 1856-1859 the range of wage differentials had narrowed, but the practice of individual contract continued to the 1870's.[4] The pay for Indian workers at the ranch, however, became standardized around 1859.[5] The Anaheim Cooperative, founded with San Francisco capital, relied primarily on Mexican and Indian labor at the wage of 50 to 75 cents per day.[6] Thus early Southern California constituted a distinct labor market on account of cheap local labor supply.

The first evidence of Chinese labor in the Southern California

ranches came in the year 1864. At that time Benjamine Davis
Wilson had nine Chinese on his payroll at $1.20 per day each.
Two more were imported from San Francisco that fall.[7]

The labor problem in the north was distressing for the agriculturists, to say the least, because of the high income of
miners, artisans, and common laborers. After the initial
boom for food producers had passed in the mid-1850's, the
high price local market became a rarity and farmers began to
calculate cost-price spread. As a result, they set the wage
scale at $30 to $40 per month[8] and took whatever laborers
made their services available. In other words, unable to
compete with high-priced labor, the agriculturists tried to
regulate their production according to the size of their labor
supply.

A typical consequence of low wages was low quality of
labor. In 1862 farmers complained: [9]

> Those who tramp through the country calling them-
> selves farm laborers, are the most complete set of
> loafing idlers to be found in any country; if a fellow
> is too lazy, too drunk or too stupid to keep himself
> alive laboring about the towns, he is good enough for
> a farm .... here they are the birds of passage... and
> they are always ready for a start, the instant they hear
> a Frazer river, a Cariboo or a Whashoe excitement.

There seemed to be no material improvement in the quality of
white agricultural labor during the 1870's.[10] Therefore, Chinese labor was indispensable for the development of agriculture in California. However, the initial attraction for the
Chinese was mining, and not until the placer mines gave out
in the mid-1860's were Chinese laborers available in any
quantity.

A. Haraszthy and his Buena Vista Vinicultural Society in
Sonoma and Napa counties were primarily responsible for the
introduction of Chinese labor to northern vineyards. At one
time in the early 1860's, 100 Chinese were employed in the
field, at $1 each per day. When they were not working for
the society, the Chinese were hired out to neighboring vineyards.[11] They were employed as harvest laborers at the same
wage rate. [12]

In the 1870's there seemed to be distinct seasonal wage scales for agricultural workers. During the winter slack season they were $22 per month for Chinese, $30 for whites, and in summer $30 for Chinese, and $40 to $50 for whites.[13]   After 1869 the wage scale for Chinese agricultural laborers in Southern California declined slightly from about $1.20 per day to 96 cents per day or $25 to $26.50 per month.[14]   If a higher wage was given, it was often accompanied by a special notation in the wage book by way of an explanation.[15]   At times, the Chinese were employed at piece work, such as picking cotton at two cents per pound. It was reported that they could average 69 pounds per day. If true, a daily wage would have been $1.38.[16]   In contrast with the wage rates of the Chinese agricultural laborers, information about the distribution of labor is extremely sketchy. Our only source is the   census returns. According to these the distribution of Chinese agricultural laborers in major farming counties is as follows.[17]

TABLE 26

CHINESE FARM LABORERS IN RURAL COUNTIES, 1870-1880

County	1870	1880
Alameda	359	825
Contra Costa	1	128
Los Angeles	12	99
Placer	25	119
Sacramento	668	218
San Joaquin	51	296
San Mateo	148	86
Santa Clara	104	689
Salano	129	174
Sonoma	9	183
Yuba	14	227
California	1,807	3,380

The number of agricultural laborers in the state by national origins for the years 1870 and 1880 are shown in Table 27.

TABLE 27

NATIONAL ORIGIN OF FARM LABORERS, 1870-1880[18]

Country	1870	1880
United States	10,203	14,597
Germany	852	890
Ireland	1,362	1,210
China	1,637	3,380
TOTAL	16,231	23,856

According to the table the vast majority of farm laborers were native Americans. However, most of them, like the majority of German and Irish workers, were regular agricultural laborers. The Chinese comprised the only group that had made a significant increase during that decade. This phenomenon can partially be explained by the fact that during this decade the rate of increase of harvest labor outstripped that of regular farm labor. The Chinese were mainly in the latter group.

Assuming the accuracy of census reports, we still have a rather inadequate source of information on migratory laborers. For the census was taken in early June at the beginning rather than at the peak of the harvest season. In 1870, as far as can be determined from the Manuscript Population Census, there were 1,500 unspecified Chinese laborers in rural California outside of the twelve major cities. By 1880 the number increased to over 4,000. As levee and reclamation labor was usually differentiated in the census, it is perhaps not too risky to assume that one-third of these unspecified laborers had been farm laborers at one time or another during the year. If so, the total number of Chinese farm laborers for the year 1870 would be 2,300 and for 1880 close to 5,000. This ranked it as a major occupation open to the Chinese next to mining and domestic service.

One of the most compelling reasons for the hiring of Chinese in agriculture was the need for cheap and abundant labor. Of the vineyards and orchards of southern California listed in the 1880 Manuscript Agricultural Census, labor cost amounted from one-fourth to one-third of the total estimated income with only two notable exceptions, one of which was the Cooperative Nursery Company of Los Angeles,[19] where presumably members performed part of the labor task. This ratio of labor-total costs came very close to modern estimates.[20]

On the other hand, only twelve of the thirty-one farms that had produced grain in excess of 4,000 bushels annually in San Joaquin County showed a labor cost equal to one-fourth of the product value in 1880. The ratio was considerably lower in others. Of the twelve, six had a large portion of unimproved land.[21] It is not unlikely that these were new farms, and that their labor cost included the expenses for clearing the land, etc.

A direct consequence of high labor cost was low investment returns. Of the vineyards and orchards in Los Angeles County, only half had a "surplus" of $1,000 for the dispensation of marketing costs, taxes, and living expenses after wage payments and the hypothetical 10 per cent interest charge on the assessed value of the land had been met.[22] Investment return was materially less than 10 per cent current interest rates, and very likely less than 4 per cent.

If the same method of calculation is applied to wheat farms in San Joaquin County, only five out of thirty-one large producers had a surplus of less than $1,500 after interest and wages had been deducted from current income. In three farms the hypothetical interest and wage combined was only equal to one-third of the total income.[23]

Moreover, agriculturists in general paid higher interest rates than urban industrialists and merchants. For instance, the Blucher Ranch business papers showed that only once between the years 1866-1869 was money borrowed at the going bank rate. On other occasions a premium of one-half of 1 per cent per month was paid.[24] Because of a low profit margin and high borrowing charges, wages remained the only cost that could be kept at a minimum level. Therefore, direct competition for labor with industry was out of the question. Cheap Chinese labor was indispensable.

Furthermore, the agricultural labor market was even more unorganized than the industrial labor market. The San Francisco labor Exchange had never been able to supply more than 2,000 workers to agriculture in any given year between 1867-1880.[25] Hence farm producers had to take positive action to secure an adequate labor supply at certain crucial periods such as planting and harvesting. Chinese labor contractors appeared to be the perfect answer to their needs. The following is a good example.[26]

> We had a very large wheat-field. It was harvest time, and the superintendent wrote down to send him up a couple hundred of white men. I went to all the labor institutions here and employed men of all kinds, of all nations. I gave them the usual country wages, whatever it was, $34 or $40 a month, I think. We had to abandon it after trying a couple of weeks, and losing a great deal of wheat by the experiment. Those men would not work more than two or three days, or a week, and they would quit. I kept the steamer here almost loaded sending up white men, but they leave as fast as I sent them. I then went to a Chinaman and told him that I wanted to contract for binding and shocking wheat. We did the reaping by machines. I made the contract at so much per acre. The weather was warm. They went up there. Several hundred of them came. We had one or two hundred acres that had been reaped, and needed putting up very badly; and the next morning it was all in shock. The Chinamen did the work that night. They did the work well and faithfully, and of course we abandoned white labor.

In addition to insuring the farmers an adequate labor force, sometimes the contractor or head men took over the supervising job. The agriculturists could devote undivided attention to other matters. Furthermore, being sure of temporary workers, the employer was able to maintain a small regular labor force. In other words, the employer gained greater freedom in regulating the size of his work force and thereby minimized his labor expenses.

As in industry, Chinese agricultural labor represented a constant unit labor cost; that is to say, an increase in demand for labor had little or no effect on wage rates. This was extremely important for the farmers during harvest time. Evidence indicates that of all labor-using enterprises in California before 1880, only the Central Pacific Railroad had to pay more than the going wage for its Chinese laborers.

As the industrialists, the agriculturists maintained that commodity price determined factor costs or wage rates; or, in their own words, "It is not the competition of Chinamen that prevents farm wages from rising, but the cost of freight to Liverpool and the price of wheat there."[27]

Because of their dependency on the Chinese labor, and their specific grievances, when the Grange first swept the state in the early spring of 1873, it was a separate and distinct movement from the urban workingmen's agitation. By the mid-1870's, however, the two found a common ground in the anti-monopoly issue. Had the leadership among the workers not been preoccupied by its anti-Chinese obsession, an anti-monopoly alliance might have been organized in California.

Farmers as a class were not committed to the expulsion of Chinese.[28] Instances of individual conversions were numerous, however, because of the family farm myth and the divergence of interests between large and small land owners. Many farmers believed that the large farms in California were mainly sustained by Chinese labor. They would have much preferred to have these farms divided into small plots of perhaps 320 acres apiece.[29] One farmer put it this way and his incoherence betrayed the strong resentment felt toward the big farmers.[30]

> If those men had not monopolized the growth of currants in large quantities by the aid of Chinese labor, even with the Chinese here and they holding their lands, those currants would be grown by men who would use their own children, their girls and boys, in picking of these currants...

As the small farmers began to join the workers in the anti-

Chinese movements, the united front of the large agriculturists weakened. The more calculating farmers might have realized that by supporting the urban anti-Chinese movement, and by limiting the job opportunities of the Chinese in the cities, more of them would have been made available on the farm. That, in turn, would have achieved a reduction of labor cost by lowering alternative cost. Others might have conceived the support of the anti-Chinese movement to be a small price for a farmer-labor alliance against the "monopoly," and the unity of the farm movement.

Consciously trying to maintain a common front against the railroad, or intimidated by the threat of violence, farm producers began to replace Chinese with white laborers in the mid-1870's. Organizations in San Francisco did their utmost to supply the agriculturists' labor needs, even to the extent of mobilizing teen-agers in the city.[31] However, enthusiasm was no substitute for experience and a self-sacrificing spirit had a definite limit. Some farmers complained that the white workers "have everything to learn when they come up to the farm."[32] Others demanded a wage ceiling that would ensure the farmers "fair average margin of profit" or required that the Chinese be permitted to work until they could "afford to hire white men by the year."[33]

Disenchantment turned into bitter resentment, when certain workers or vagrants resorted to direct action in the form of willful destruction of property. Numerous cases of incendiary fires in grain fields, stacks and barns were reported in 1877.[34] After that the break between the farmers and the workers was inevitable. The Alta California commented:[35]

> City agitators who have wakened this echo of incendiarism in the farming districts are some of the men whose help was solicited by the resolutions of the State Grange, when it proposed to unite the farmers and workingmen in a new political deal.... The Grangers took part in starting an agitation with a communistic tendency, though most of them had no intention or desire to do injustice, much less violence, and now it begins to react upon them. It is easier to kindle a fire than to stop it.

In his brilliant Ph.D. dissertation, <u>Sectionalism and the California Constitution of 1879</u>, Dudley Morehead demonstrated with conclusive evidence that the farmers wrested the control of the constitutional convention from both the industrialists (and the monopoly), and the workers, and that farm votes rather than urban votes ensured the ratification of the 1879 constitution. [36]

External pressures notwithstanding, the Chinese continued to work on California's farms during the 1880's. Even the processing industries, which mainly used white labor, realized the continuous operation of their plants depended upon the availability of Chinese harvest labor in the fields.[37] California's fruit industry has been primarily dependent upon foreign cheap labor to this day. It has seen racial origins of the laborers change during the past seventy years, but not the basic economic consideration.

CHAPTER VI

INDUSTRIES: WOOLEN TEXTILE AND CLOTHING

Part I: Woolen Factories

Woolen mills were the first factories of any size to appear in California. Capital requirements limited the field to a few large firms: three, and then two in San Francisco, two in San Jose, and one each in Sacramento, Marysville, Stockton and Los Angeles. Without a substantial lead in technology, such other advantages as economies of scale, were insufficient for the British and Eastern factories to offset tariff and distribution costs and thereby maintain a pre-eminent position in California. As business expanded, partly on army contract, California woolen goods even invaded the national market.

The woolen factories were among the first in California to conform to the national pattern in business cycles. While other industries were still in their infancy, supplying primarily local markets, the woolen mills of San Francisco had already gone through the process of wartime overexpansion and postwar contraction. In 1867 the mills were only operating at 50 per cent of capacity in California when the workers proclaimed that Chinese labor was the primary cause of unemployment and wage reduction. The employers maintained that cheap labor was indispensable to the survival of the industry, and indirectly the continued employment of white workers in these factories.[1] In a word, with the first recession, Chinese labor inevitably became a major issue in industrial dispute.

Although California mills had installed modern machinery at their outset no major technological innovations were made between the 1860's and 1880's. Furthermore, the decline of the national price level in woolen goods had been much slower and at a lesser magnitude than the general price level. The

most important products of California mills, woolen textile
suiting, experienced a price drop of 51 per cent, while blankets
and flannels met one of 11 per cent from 1865 to 1879. The
general price level declined 64 per cent in the same period. [2]
As the major cause of business failures in California was the
inability to compete in price, this point is most important.

In the absence of other reliable data, raw material input
is our best index to business conditions, and the raw material
labor input ratio, or the quantity of wool consumed per worker,
is the best gauge of under-employment. Table 28 was taken and
computed from San Francisco Municipal Reports.

Except for the 1879-1880 season, fluctuations or production
in woolen textiles in California, as reflected in the number of
pounds of wool consumed, conformed punctiliously with levels
of business activity in the nation. Under-employment became
a serious problem after the 1874-1875 season and preceded
a reduction in the labor force by a year. The low raw material-
labor input ratio in the late 1870's was due to a shift in line
of products, depressed business conditions, and the replace-
ment of women for Chinese labor in some departments. The
high cost of labor turnover was the price paid by many employers at the height of the anti-Chinese agitations. Analyzing
the development of the woolen industry, John S. Hittel concluded that the major impediments to its rapid growth were the
scarcity of capital, low investment return, and uncertainty of
labor, while labor was thought to be "too high in price, too
scarce in its supply, and too unreliable in its character."[3]

The heritage of the Gold Rush died hard. Capital was absorbed by mining and trade. High borrowing charges and wages
cut down the profit margin. Employment at a fixed wage was
looked upon with disdain, and was regarded by many as a
stop-gap job between gold rushes. Ex-miners submitted to
industrial discipline both with great difficulty and reluctance.
Industry and railroads both turned to the same alternative—
Chinese labor. Woolen mills were the pioneers in this experiment for industry.

Because of this fact the woolen mills were founded on Chinese labor; white workers, outside of foremen, were a rarity
in the early 1860's. Because business was expanding, conflicts

TABLE 28

WOOLEN INDUSTRY IN SAN FRANCISCO, 1866-1881[4]

	Number of Workers Employed	Number of Pounds of wool Consumed	Number of Pounds of Wool Consumed per Worker
1866-67	725	3,500,000	4,800
1867-68	750	3,000,000	4,000
1868-69	750	3,250,000	4,200
1869-70		Data incomplete	
1870-71	825	2,800,000	3,390
1871-72	840	3,700,000	4,400
1872-73	870	4,000,000	4,600
1873-74	900	4,500,000	5,000
1874-75	900	3,150,000	3,500
1875-76	700	2,500,000	3,570
1876-77	600	2,200,000	3,666
1877-78	700	2,200,000	3,140
1878-79	700	2,200,000	3,140
1879-80	700	2,200,000	3,140
1880-81	819	3,000,000	3,750

between white and Chinese labor were not in evidence. The first anti-Chinese incident came with the 1867 recession. As in the case of the miner's strike of 1869-1871, the textile workers failed to win the support of the press. In one of its editorials, the Alta California bitterly attacked the "prejudiced, ignorant" natives who "blindly agitated against the employment of Chinese labor by which alone the mills could continue in operation."[5] However, the recession was short in duration and anti-Chinese sentiment again subsided for some time.

Chinese labor in the woolen mills in San Francisco in the late 1860's was estimated at between 400 and 500.[6] During the early 1870's it expanded with the size of the total labor force reaching about 600 or 700,[7] and remaining 73 to 80 per cent of the total labor force. Major reductions in Chinese labor came in the 1875-1876 season when a general business downswing began and anti-Chinese agitation gained wide support.[8] After that, the mills were successful usually in resisting external pressure to further reduce Chinese labor.

Factories, in contrast with sweatshops, have a high degree of division of labor. Immediate dismissal of all Chinese would have meant stoppage of operations in the whole plant, not just a reduction of production proportionate to a cut in the labor force. Management attempted to explain this and other factors— that some work was too heavy for the females, that it took too long to teach the girls, that the company could not afford this, and that there were not enough female workers.[9] But the most interesting reason given is that the employment of Chinese labor assured a degree of continuity in production by checking strikes. This enabled the firm to secure loans from banks because of the reduced risk.[10] However, as in the case of mining, the best assurance against strikes was a mixed labor force. As Robert Peckham testified on the Chinese, "I mean that they will combine. They have the power of combining. If you do not happen to get along with them and have a difficulty with one, the whole lot will stand up for each other, and as a general thing go together."[11]

Wages for the Chinese and the females depended on types of work as well as the ratio of labor cost. In the blankets and flannel division, where labor costs amounted to 25 per cent of the total costs, the Chinese were paid 95 cents a day, and the girls $1.25. In the tweed suit division, where labor costs equaled only 13 per cent of the total costs, both were paid $1.50.[12] Wage rates for the Chinese and females in Marysville were comparable to that of San Francisco. In Sacramento and Stockton the pay seemed to be a little lower, while white males got a uniform wage of $2.50 in all factories.[13] Further gradation of pay, according to types of jobs and skill came only in the 1880's. In spite of repeated prophecies on the part of employers, wage differentials between San Francisco and the Eastern states had not seriously impaired their competitive position. Not until the depression of 1886 were Eastern manufacturers able to undersell local producers because of the disparity of costs.[14] However, in other related industries such as clothing, where sweatshops dominated, in California the competition of Eastern imports was immediately felt in the mid-1870's.   By the 1870's these related industries had also conditioned the role of Chinese labor as well.

Part II: Clothing

The clothing industry quickly had become well known for "cut-throat" competition among numerous small manufacturers. It was characterized also by its highly seasonal nature of marketing and employment. This was especially true for California; according to H. H. Bancroft no organized clothing factories could be said to have existed in San Francisco before 1880.[1]   The degree of seasonal fluctuations must be inferred from the daily wage rate, the size of the labor force, and the total annual labor cost of a multitude of small firms. Figures arrived at through such calculations indicate the same amplitude of seasonal variations for the industry in California as in Massachusetts. The estimates are 32 weeks of employment for ready-made and 24 weeks for custom-trade clothing manufacturing.[2]

The California Gold Rush was one of the major factors that stimulated the growth of the ready-made clothing industry in the East.   These dominated the California market as late as 1880.   Even in 1870 the census recorded only 757 workers in 177 clothing "factories."[3] Shirt manufacturing was not listed separately in the census, but both clothing and shirt making in California progressed steadily between 1870 and 1876. The great increase in the number of workers employed in the 1876-1877 season was not matched by a corresponding increase in the value of the product or a comparable price drop. A sudden increase of labor force, moderate increases in production, and a sharp reduction in the number of firms as concurrent responses to a recession were phenomena of California's clothing industries.

During the second half of the 1870's, smaller clothing manufacturers in San Francisco enjoyed the advantage of decreasing labor costs, which was denied to most other industries. As women with sewing machines worked at a minimal pay, [4] whatever price cuts the smaller manufacturers were able to offer could be matched by the clothing wholesalers. They "assisted" the Chinese in setting up their shops by supplying them with materials and by purchasing their finished products. Judging from the meager income of the Chinese co-operatives, these wholesalers could well afford to make price cuts. San Francisco Municipal Reports are the best source on the general development of the clothing industry in this period.

TABLE 29[5]

CLOTHING INDUSTRY IN SAN FRANCISCO, 1870-1881

Number of Firms		Number of Workers	Value of Product	Value of Product Per Worker
1870-1871	7	98	$ 271,000	$2,764
1871-1872	10	156	300,000	1,923
1872-1873	12	193	400,000	2,072
1873-1874	10	164	365,000	2,225
1874-1875	8	422	730,000	1,756
1875-1876	22	650	1,020,000	1,569
1876-1877	10	3,500	2,000,000	571
1877-1878	12	4,000	3,000,000	750
1878-1879	12	4,000	3,000,000	750
1879-1880	12	4,200	3,150,000	750
1880-1881	12	4,800	3,662,500	759

The value of product per worker in the first half of the 1870's was unusually high, an indication that local producers were to be found primarily in high price fields. After 1874, as the value of products rose and the labor force steadily increased, the value of product per worker declined. Implicitly, local manufacturers entered the low price field and Eastern competition became intense.

In the ready-made trade, Chinese firms and laborers dominated. A major complaint of the day about the Chinese laborers was their strong desire for self-employment. A Chinese would often serve as apprentice and journeyman at $6 to $20 per month for a short period to acquire the necessary skill and capital to open his own shop.[6] It was reported that as soon as a Chinese learned his trade, he would fall sick, and recommend another Chinese to take his place. When the latter became familiar with his work, sickness promptly overtook him, and so on and so on.

In spite of this labor turnover, some employers still claimed they could net a dollar per day per worker on Chinese labor over what they were able to make with white workers.[8] Not until business failures mounted during the mid-1870's was Chinese labor considered a threat to American economic welfare, nor did the anti-Chinese movement gain support from the shopowners and the press. Not until the small shopowners joined the anti-Chinese crusade in the mid-1870's did the movement become a formidable political force. By that date clothing manufacturers were at the forefront of the anti-Chinese movement because they were conscious of Chinese competition in their fields.

The reason for the employment of Chinese labor in clothing manufacturing was the same as in any other industry—the scarcity of labor. Two out of three applicants were Chinese.[9] But more specifically, employers complained about the lack of skilled female labor and the high cost of training. One observer counseled greater patience with white female workers in the initial period of training, explaining that the Chinese worked from infancy and were, therefore, accustomed to work and able to pick up a new skill immediately.[10]

In general, adjustment to industrial discipline was a slow and painful process for women in San Francisco. The ease of transfer or mobility from home to factory was vastly exaggerated in the expectation and pronouncements of the general public. Sewing at home and garment making in a "factory" were two different and distinct processes. Factory jobs demanded standardization, emphasized simple, repetitive motions with a definite work rhythm. Mastering the process of button-holing, hemming, or finishing meant acquiring an entirely new work pattern. In addition, the work was dictated by the rhythms of the machine and not by human individuality. The Chinese had a new but simple process to learn while women had a great deal to unlearn. Furthermore, a factory was not a sewing session, where social functions dominated. Girls were prone to gossip and slowing down in one division held up the whole production or occasioned possible waste of material. These were luxuries the employers could ill afford.

The rise of the clothing industry in California served as an example for obsolescence of skill or changes in production and consumption patterns as a result of technological innovation. The first victim was fancy needle work. Females capable of exquisitely fine needle work had been doing well in San Francisco; but by the mid-1870's the public taste had changed and the current recession had hastened its decline. Someone remarked with bewilderment and bitterness that the people seemed to be "infatuated" with the Chinese. Whatever work was being done was sent to them while women with remarkable skills were half starving. [11]

Sewing machines and sweatshops took the manufacturing of shirts, blouses, underwear, dresses and suits out of private homes. As a result the art of making a whole garment was downgraded. Shoddy or mended undergarments underneath lavish and expensive gowns and dresses soon became a thing of the past. Trade in these lines quickly expanded. With a strong urge for self employment, the Chinese took up cigar and clothing manufacturing, industries which had low capital requirements, with gusto and alacrity. Used to strict discipline at home though with no previous experience in garment making, the Chinese laborers adapted to sweatshop work with ease.

The coming of popular magazines with patterns in fashion offered still another job opportunity for the Chinese. Women often picked out a pattern and hired a Chinese operator to run the machine at home. As a result, many tailor shops lost their exclusive clientele. Thus one of the owners who had at various times offered to hire out her female employees found that the ladies seemed to prefer Chinese and "would not take a girl at any price." [12] Patterns enabled women of modest means to follow the whims of fashion. Chinese sewing-machine operators, being new in the field, were perhaps more pliable to the directions and specifications of the pattern and the wishes of their patrons.

The entry of Chinese firms into clothing manufacturing dated from the late 1860's. By the mid-1870's, at the time of the major price drop, the Chinese were accused of monopolizing the underwear and overall trades. Firms which formerly had been engaged in these fields had diversified their products, had shifted to other branches of the industry, or had entered into fields of specialized products.[13] Data on wage rates, market conditions, and the degree and extent of Eastern and local competitions for these sub-industries, however, is lacking.

In men and women's clothing industry the average size of the firms in California was smaller than the ones in New York and Massachusetts. This is reflected in the figures in the numbers of workers per firm, and average capital per firm. The higher fixed capital per worker ratio occurred in the women's clothing industry and in 1880 in men's clothing as results of smaller firms, rather than as results of a higher degree of capital intensification. Again, the wage rates in California were higher due in part to the preponderance of female workers in the East. Higher wage rates did not seem to have impaired their profit margin.[14]

However, because of the numerous sub-industries within the men's and women's clothing industries, the average gross income and variable cost or wage ratios meant very little. As in the case of the cigar industry, California firms were not competing with the average firms in New York or Massachusetts but with those dominating the national markets.

The Chinese entered into the clothing industry fairly late. There were two Chinese clothing shops recorded in the 1870 Manuscript Products of Industry Census, employing 16 males, one female, and one minor.[15] The gross income-variable cost ratio was 1.44, much higher than the average firms in California. However, these shops could not have operated a full twelve months at the time of the census taking. Thus the seasonal nature of profit and employment was minimized, if not totally absent.

In 1880, the fact that several hundreds of Chinese were working under contract for wholesalers[16] after being discharged in the late 1870's, further complicated the situation. Only in a few fair sized shops were the wage rates of from $3 to $4 per day for male workers and $2 to $3 for female workers maintained. They were mostly in the custom trade which was highly seasonal. Taking the total wage and dividing it by the number of workers times daily wages, we may assume that workers in these shops were employed from 22 to 30 weeks in the 1879-1880 season. One of the firms employing Chinese exclusively at $2 a day, appears to have operated at full capacity for 300 days and paid 50 workers $30,000 for the census year 1880. [17]

In the fields where Eastern competition was intense, the wages paid to Chinese and females were between $1 and $1.50 per day. Because of the low profit margin, such industries as ladies' underwear or overalls were left to the Chinese after the mid-1870's. Imports from the East were reduced to a trickle. [18] In these trades it could have been assumed that the expulsion of Chinese would conceivably raise employment if enough skilled females could be found. However, even the more profitable branches in the clothing industry suffered from the scarcity of skilled labor, especially females.

In the clothing industry in San Francisco, including shirt making, the number of Chinese had been estimated as high as 3,250,[19] and as low as 1,230[20] in 1876. As there was no evidence of a mass exit of Chinese workers between 1876-1880, the number must lie somewhere between 2,000 and 2,500. In 1880 the Manuscript Population Census showed that there were 661 working for clothing manufacturers in San Francisco, 156 overall makers, 67 underwear makers, 580 shirt makers, and 114 sewing machine operators.[21] If we include tailors and seamstresses, the total number of Chinese in the clothing industry in San Francisco during 1880 would appear to have been no more than 2,000.

*   *   *   *

By comparison, shirt "factories" in California were smaller. Their wage rates and proportionate wage expenditures were higher, and their profit lower than that in the East. Perhaps in no other industry can the unfavorable competitive position of the firms in California be so conclusively illustrated by the averages alone, as the following table shows: [22]

TABLE 30

COMPARISONS BETWEEN THE SHIRT INDUSTRY IN CALIFORNIA, NEW YORK, AND MASSACHUSETTS, 1880

	California	New York	Massachusetts
Capital per firm	$3,400	$19,143	$7,502
Workers per firm	13.8	79	25.1
Fixed capital per labor	$ 249	$ 270	$ 300
Wage-material cost ratio	55%	42.5%	34%
Gross income-variable cost ratio	1.22	1.37	1.29
Wage	$ 239	$ 190	$ 221

Shirt manufacturing depended primarily on Chinese workers. As in the case of the clothing industry, female laborers were in most cases inexperienced. After relating one of his unfortunate experiments with females, one shirt manufacturer remarked bitterly: "Among all those unemployed women, it seems strange that there are none competent to make shirts. Well, but it is so."[23]

The development of shirt manufacturing paralleled that of the clothing industry, as shown in Table 31.[24]

It witnessed the same sudden influx of labor in the 1876-1877 season. But Eastern competition in shirt making, where products were homogeneous, was even more intense than in other branches. Diversification and specialization on the part of California shops were not practicable. Therefore, in the next season, 1877-1878, there was the mass exit of workers and drastic curtailment of production followed.

Shirt manufacturing in California passed through a full circle in its methods of production. In the mid-1860's shirts were made by women, who took orders from shops, supplied their own materials and worked at home. Then wholesalers, in the late 1860's, began to hire Chinese to do piece work, supplying them with materials.[25]   By the end of the 1860's, the putting-out system was superseded by sweatshops. In the late 1870's, however, many Chinese shirt makers were again

TABLE 31

SHIRT INDUSTRY IN SAN FRANCISCO, 1871-1881

Year	Number of Firms	Number of Workers	Value of Product	Value of Product Per Worker
1871-1872	3	60	$ 18,000	300
1872-1873	6	130	55,000	423
1873-1874	7	145	120,000	827
1874-1875	8	743	798,000	1,074
1875-1876	8	640	650,000	1,015
1876-1877	8	2,000	1,000,000	500
1877-1878	6	1,000	500,000	500
1878-1879	20	1,000	500,000	500
1879-1880	20	1,000	470,000	470
1880-1881	-	1,000	500,000	454

under contract to the wholesalers, though they nominally founded their own co-operatives.

Such sweatshops were still in their infancy in 1870. The Manuscript Product of Industry Census listed five such firms which employed 46 workers. The annual income of female workers was about $300 in shops employing girls and minors exclusively. If the wages of female workers in other shops stood at the same level, seven male workers earned $457 each, one $1,000, and two $1,500. The latter seemed to have been executives or supervisors.[26] The income-variable cost ratio was 1.44—sure evidence that profits in clothing were quite high in 1870.

Between 1876 and 1880, the daily wage of skilled females and Chinese was cut from $1.25 and $1.10 to $1.00, and that for minors from 90 cents to 50 to 75 cents.[27] Wage reduction probably came at the 1877-1878 season, or possibly the previous year. Value of product per worker had declined from $1,015 in the 1875-1876 season to $500 in the next season since there had been an influx of workers during 1876-1877. Those who were regularly employed probably produced more

than $500 worth of shirts. In 1877-1878, however, workers
were leaving the industry. The remaining workers made less
than $500 worth of products. Under this depressed condition,
it may be presumed that wage cuts took place. Even at this
low wage rate, however, many larger firms were on the verge
of bankruptcy. [28]

The 1880 Manuscript Manufacture Census shows that the
annual earnings of shirt makers in Chinese firms was $240,
slightly higher than those in other firms, which seemed to show
a higher degree of seasonality. Average earnings of Chinese
shirt makers under contract to wholesalers appeared to be the
highest in the trade, ranging from $200 to $300 per year. [29]
However, as "independent producers," other expenses such
as taxes, rent, and machinery rentals had to be met.

Because of the low profit margin, in no other industry was
the need for female and Chinese labor more urgent and imperative. As skilled females were not available in quantity, about
80 per cent of the shirt makers were Chinese. [30] Thus shirt
manufacturing offers another example of Eastern competition
setting price levels in San Francisco. Through price, it influenced maximum wage level, entry, and lastly, employment.
For instance, Eastern shirts of a cheaper grade were sold in
San Francisco at $9.50 per dozen. At this price level local
manufacturers could afford to pay $2.60 per dozen for labor as
the maximum wage. Since skilled labor could earn more in
other sewing works, this type of shirt was not produced. Entry
was zero, and employment was zero. Therefore employment
was limited to the high price fields. The firing of Chinese
would not solve the problems of unemployment unless higher
wages and prices increased the sales of its product. In actuality expulsion only resulted in a return to the putting-out system, and thereby benefitted the wholesalers. About one-third
of the Chinese shirt makers were under contract to such wholesalers by 1880.

Obviously, the main problems in shirt making in California
were tied to technological and organizational lags. Sweatshop
production was on its way out. White and Chinese employers
and employees were competing in a diminishing market. With
cheap Eastern shirts sold at $9.50 per dozen, those made by

Chinese were priced at $15 and by whites at $21.[31]   The only plausible salvation for the white manufacturers and workers would have been total exclusion of Eastern import in addition to the expulsion of the Chinese.   To do so California would have had to secede from the Union.

Another and the most urgent problem in the clothing industry was the scarcity of capital investment. Eastern manufacturers, with newer equipment and a greater division of labor could in some cases pay higher wages than their counterparts in San Francisco. [32] The scarcity of capital, in other words, retarded the transition from sweatshop to factory production in California. As a result the expanding market was taken over by Eastern industrialists without even a token challenge from San Francisco. Chinese firms specializing in ladies underwear or overalls held on a little longer, but their profit margin and wages were cut to the minimum level by 1880 because of price competition. Capital intensive production methods were to triumph alike over the rebellion of the whites, and the endurance of the Chinese. California could not remain a separate economic region. It became an integral part of an emerging national market in the 1870's and 1880's.

CHAPTER VII

INDUSTRIES: SHOE, CIGAR, AND FRINGE INDUSTRIES

Part I: Shoe Manufacturing

The Gold Rush was also one of the major impetuses in the rapid development of shoe manufacturing factories in the East, especially in Massachusetts.[1] The sudden extension of trade, the inflated demand, and the necessity of meeting delivery deadlines demanded a greater degree of production control and a speed-up greater than the putting-out system could provide. Eastern imports were to dominate the California market to the late 1860's when local manufacturing established its foothold. Thereafter imports never approached the prewar level despite the prodigious population growth that transpired.

If the fluctuations in California's woolen industry closely resembled national trade cycles, the shoe industry on the west coast was much more heterogeneous and complex. Aside from a few "factories," it was composed of a multitude of small sweatshops. Production, marketing and profit patterns often times ran contrary to the national trend. Moreover, the diversity of such shops defied uniformity or certainty in classification. Data from different sources often offered no basis for comparison.

In terms of the size of the labor force, and the value of the product, the shoe industry in California reached its peak in late 1877. However, the value of the product per worker started to decline in late 1874, reaching its lowest level in early 1879. The following was taken from the San Francisco Municipal Reports (Table 32).

Obviously the value of product per worker in the shoe industry was unusually high in the first half of the 1870's. This

TABLE 32

SHOE MANUFACTURING IN SAN FRANCISCO, 1869-1881[2]

	Number of Firms	Number of Workers	Value of Product	Value of Product Per Worker
1869-1870	6	660	$ 602,259	$ 912
1870-1871	5	702	1,205,000	1,710
1871-1872	31	1,841	2,536,700	1,380
1872-1873	35	2,000	3,000,000	1,500
1873-1874	18	1,200	2,275,000	1,900
1874-1875	20	2,000	2,793,000	1,367
1875-1876	26	2,500	2,900,000	1,160
1876-1877	-	3,000	3,000,000	1,000
1877-1878	56	3,000	2,000,000	666
1878-1879	56	2,900	1,780,000	614
1879-1880	56	2,700	1,675,000	620
1880-1881	56	2,400	1,580,000	658

was due to the high percentage of boots produced and the high cost of raw material input. The recession in 1873-1874 was due primarily to an upsurge of imports which followed the panic, depression and price decline in the East. Incidentally, at this time, under pressure of this competition and the labor movement, a number of firms introduced child labor as a substitute for Chinese labor.[3]

The decline of product value per worker, and the subsequent fall of total value of product were due to a variety of factors. The postwar period was characterized by a deflationary trend, but for the shoe industry in California it became a matter of crucial importance only in the second half of the 1870's. In 1875, although gold prices in terms of greenbacks showed an upward trend, the price of leather and footwear fell suddenly. In the year 1878, the gold price fell only slightly and in 1879 the United States returned to the gold standard, but the price of shoes continued a persistent downward trend.

The following table illustrates the timing and magnitude of
the declines in gold price, shoe price, and the value of footwear product per worker in San Francisco.

TABLE 33

DEFLATIONARY TREND IN FOOTWEAR, 1874-1880[4]

Year	Price Index of Leather and Footwear	Price Index of Gold	Value of Product Per Worker in San Francisco
1874	152	111.4	$1,376
1875	141.2	114.9	1,160
1876	135.5	111.5	1,000
1877	137.2	104.8	666
1878	124.4	104.8	614
1879	120.0	100	620
1880	122.2	100	658

With a time lag of six months, the value of products per worker
in general conformed with the trend of the national price level,
with minor exceptions. In the year 1877 the national price for
shoes went up. In terms of money, however, productivity
dropped drastically during the 1877-1878 season in California.
This inconsistency resulted from a change in product emphasis,
from boots to shoes, in San Francisco.

There is ample ground for the belief that this change was
underway when the recession of 1876 began. However, the
downswing was not immediately perceptible in either the size
of labor force or in the total value of product. Only in the ratio
between the two—the value of product per worker—was it evident. Production and employment increased but prices declined.
Many of the discharged Chinese laborers entered into the employment of Chinese firms. Others formed co-operatives or
partnerships as contemporaries called them. These shops seldom made boots.

The fall in product value per worker would have been the

more striking had it not been for the fact that certain white workers formed co-operatives to combat the recession. These co-operatives, in turn, did a most prosperous business in boots.[5] The existing unit price differential was $2.50—$2.00 for a pair of shoes and $4.50 for boots.[6] The full impact of product change was not appreciable until 1877. Product change, in turn, entailed a degree of work stoppage and thereby further accentuated the deterioration of product value per worker ratio. Moreover, the sweatshops were notorious for their inability or unwillingness to adjust swiftly the labor force to sales variation. It is regrettable that the relative importance of the two, product change and under-employment, cannot be fully assessed for lack of reliable data.

The employment of Chinese in shoe-manufacturing can be attributed, in part, to their availability and their manual skill.[7] They had been brought into the largest shoe factory, Buckingham & Hecht, during the 1869 strike and other factories had followed suit.[8] The Chinese had been engaged in slipper manufacturing even earlier. The 1869 entry, however, is important as the first instance in which the relationship between the completion of the Central Pacific and the mass entry of Chinese in industry can be inferred. Woolen and cigar manufacturing competed with the Central Pacific for labor between 1865 and 1867.

Though the required operating capital was quite high in the shoe industry, the chief tool of production, the McKay sewing machine, was leased to manufacturers.[9] Therefore, people with limited capital could achieve the status of self employment. As a result a number of sweatshops came to be owned by Chinese in the 1870's. A manager of a leading shoe factory commented that the best Chinese workers would remain only until they had thoroughly learned the business.[10] Others stated that the Chinese were "quick to pick up the main features of the trade, and then by way of reciprocating the kindness of their white employers in instructing them, they started factories of their own and began to undersell the white labor factories."[11] Thus in the shoe industry the existence of Chinese-owned sweatshops became the foundation for a united front between labor and management against the Chinese.

However, the degree of competition has been greatly exaggerated. First of all, Eastern imports set price levels in California and Chinese and white shops competed only within this framework. Secondly, there were product and job differentiations between the white and the Chinese firms as early as 1870. Of the 2,501 shoe makers in California in 1870, only 392 were Chinese.[12] Of these, 182 were slipper makers according to the Manuscript Population Census. Moreover, a considerable portion of the remaining were in ladies' and boys' boot or shoe manufacturing. White shops and workers shunned these because of their low price and profit margin.

The 1860 Manufacturing Census reported 70 boot and shoe shops in California employing 113 workers. The average size of labor force per form was 1.6 workers.[13] The total number of workers in the field precluded substantial competition with Eastern factory-made goods. Even in 1867, when the woolen mills in California were adversely affected by the postwar economic downswing, the leading boot and shoe shops in San Francisco—Buckington and Hecht, Wentworth and Hobart, H. M. Beers, and the Pacific, were little more than sweatshops, catering to high price, custom-made trade and using very little machinery.[14] In other words, true competition with Eastern products coincided with the mass entry of Chinese workers in the late 1860's.

By 1870 the increase in labor force in the boot and shoe industries was tenfold and the value of products was twelve times greater than in 1860. Most of the gains had presumably been made in the last two or three years.

TABLE 34

COMPARISONS OF CAPITAL AND LABOR FORCE PER FIRM IN SHOE INDUSTRIES, 1870[15]

State	Capital per firm	Fixed Capital per worker	Number of Workers per Firm
California	$1,166	$321	3.0
Massachusetts	8,333	358	23.5
New York	2,285	331	5.8

Table 34 indicates that the emergence of a few "factories," or large sweatshops in California in no way changed the basic nature of the shoe industry. Of the three states, only the factories in Massachusetts had been "mechanized" by 1870. Mechanization itself increased only the capital investment per firm and not necessarily the fixed capital-labor ratio. This is explained in part by the leasing of machinery previously mentioned. The industry in California as a whole was characterized by high product price, moderate wage rates, high labor expenses and high investment return. Only a minority of the firms were in direct competition with Eastern imports.

TABLE 35

COMPARISONS OF WAGE LEVELS AND COSTS
IN SHOE INDUSTRIES, 1870[16]

	Average Annual Wage	Wage-Raw Material Input Ratio	Gross Income Variable Costs Ratio
California	$412	68%	1.34
Massachusetts	497	53%	1.12
New York	438	58%	1.38

In both California and New York custom made trade predominated; both showed a higher profit margin. Whatever adverse effect was suffered by California firms from the competition of Eastern imports was due more to a shift in consumer preference, therefore the expulsion of the Chinese could not change the pattern of indirect competition between the products of Massachusetts and California. Thus the sales and profits of the majority of the shops in California were influenced indirectly and not by the direct competition of imports or goods produced by Chinese labor.

Because of the heterogeneous nature of the boot and shoe shops in 1870, however, average figures can sometimes be quite misleading. For instance, the average annual earnings per worker for the industry as a whole in California was somewhat lower than that for Massachusetts; but the average wage for smaller shops primarily in the custom-made trade, was in some categories twice the computed average for the industry.[16] It was also higher than the average for 1860, when all the shops were engaged in custom-made trade. This offers further evidence that the main threat to the prosperity of the boot and shoe industry on the Pacific coast was the declining market and consequently employment in the custom-made trade.

Product specialization in the boot and shoe industry in California existed as early as 1870. In general, "factories" with large Chinese labor forces were mainly producing cheaper boots and shoes, with low wage rates and substantial profits. "Factories"—the larger sweatshops—with predominant white labor were found in the high price fields, with high wages and low returns. Smaller sweatshops had still higher product value per worker ratios, but with lower wage rates and modest profits. They were also in the custom-made trade.

Judging from the size of the labor force of one to ten workers, a large number of the smaller shops were in the custom trade. In the mid-1870's the survival of these was threatened not by

TABLE 36

COMPARISONS OF SHOE MANUFACTURERS IN CALIFORNIA, 1870[17]

	Value of Product per Worker	Average Annual Wage	Gross Income Variable Cost Ratio
Factory or shops with Chinese labor	$1,506	$311	1.66
Shops with white labor	2,094	904	1.12
Smaller shops with white labor*	2,463	715	1.21

*Random sample

Chinese competition but by the diminishing market for high priced boots.   They were victims of a changing consumption pattern instead of cheap labor.   Indeed, the 1870 Manuscript Product of Industry Census listed only one Chinese firm in boot making.   That one specialized in ladies' boots and apparently had not been in operation for a full year.   It had, however, an unbelievable gross income-variable cost ratio of 3.20 with a possible profit rate of 280 per cent or more. [18]

Through a unique event, Chinese competition was even felt outside the Californian labor market.   During the 1870 North Adams strike, 101 Chinese shoe makers were recruited from California and transported to Massachusetts.[19]   The threat of Chinese labor competition became more than a local concern.[20]

There seemed to be considerable discontent among the Chinese laborers in the shoe factories at the time.   In the early spring of 1873 two of the largest factories in San Francisco advertised in newspapers for boys to fill positions vacated by the Chinese.[21]   One factory spokesman stated in an interview at a later date that the Chinese had conducted several strikes against his firm.[22]

The entry of Chinese firms into shoe manufacturing was a late phenomenon.   The 1875-1876 San Francisco tax assessment listed only 8 Chinese factories, all with very modest capital.   In 1880 the number had increased to 48.[23]   Therefore, it may be concluded that the majority of Chinese firms in shoe making were established after the mass discharge of Chinese labor in 1876.   It follows inevitably that intensive competition between Chinese and American firms was a result, and not a cause, of discriminatory measures.   The expulsion of Chinese labor had not been a very effective device to better the job and income possibilities of white laborers in some sweatshops.

In mid-year 1876, Einstein   Brothers, Boot and Shoe Importers and Manufacturers, began to replace Chinese laborers. Within a few months the firm claimed to employ exclusively white laborers.[25]   Some 120 girls and 80 boys had been secured, and the females were considered superior to the Chinese in skill and efficiency.

Thus, it appears that shoe "factories" in the mid-1870's had considerable freedom in the combination of various laborers, white male, female, minor and Chinese. According to the list in the Report of the Joint Special Committee to Investigate Chinese Immigration, one firm had employed 4 white males and 10 boys, another 5 whites and 15 girls, and a third had 4 whites and 6 girls. [26] A very uneconomical labor input ratio appears to have existed, if the $2.88 daily wage for the white male workers is considered. Even apart from that, these firms had labor forces that were too small to achieve an efficient division of labor. It was not surprising that none survived the 1878 price drop. [27] The most striking feature of the above mentioned list was the high ratio of female labor: 351 females, 397 white males, 130 boys, and 470 Chinese. [28] Assuming this to have been a complete list, though evidence points to the contrary, the total number in the female labor force was still cut almost in half by 1880 from 351 to 181. [29]

This apparently paradoxical contraction in the female labor force can be explained partially as an effect of income on labor supply. As income declines in the business downswing, females enter the labor market. Conversely, when income rises during recovery, they withdraw from the market. It is reasonable to assume that the general improvement in the economy in 1880 hastened the exit of female workers.

The exit of females could deal a crushing blow to a firm employing a sizable number of female workers. Einstein & Bros. was such a firm. However, evidence seems to indicate the firm had discontinued its manufacturing division before the 1880 business upswing. Although it still retained its old name of the firm—Einstein & Bros. Boot and Shoe Importer and Manufacturer—and appeared in the San Francisco directory proper as late as 1880, it was not listed in the business directory as a boot and shoe manufacturer after 1878. [30] Neither can the name be located in the Manuscript Manufacture Census of 1880. It is entirely possible to believe boot manufacturing, still prosperous in 1876, was no longer so in 1878. The firm well may have decided to close up the "factory" and to concentrate upon retailing imports. Other firms, however, did not make the same adjustment but instead began to produce shoes. Thereafter these encountered both Eastern and local competition since Chinese manufacturers were already in the field.

Once again, however, the white firms chose to manufacture higher price lines.

The 1880 Manufacturing Census presented two sets of figures, one including 535 firms, the other 81 larger establishments. As might have been expected, the latter resembled closely output in Massachusetts, where there were some 1, 311 shops of which large ones were dominant.

TABLE 37

COMPARISONS OF SHOE INDUSTRIES, 1880[31]

	California		Massachusetts
	535 Firms	81 Firms	
Capital per firm	$2, 415	$111, 111	$16, 229
Workers per firm	5. 5	30. 8	47. 5
Fixed capital per labor	$ 430	$ 400	$ 341
Wage-raw material input ratio	68%	30. 8%	42%
Gross income-variable costs ratio	1. 23	1. 18	1. 13
Average annual wage	$ 434	$ 426	$ 341

It is evident that the larger shops in California had lower wage rates, lower wage expenses in relation to raw material expenditures, and a lower profit margin. Though average fixed capital per firm was high, fixed capital per labor was lower. This seems to suggest that larger firms with leased machinery had even a more favorable capital-labor input ratio. The larger shops presumably put a large portion of their product into competition with Eastern imports.   Thus they showed a smaller profit margin despite the lower wage rate. This is another indication that Eastern imports determined the upper limits of local profit and wage.

The data in the printed census, however, is far from adequate

for analysis.   The manuscript census returns are the primary
source of information. California shoe manufacturers, according to the 1880 Manuscript Manufacture Census, can be divided into seven major groups: (1) the factories which were
characterized by a high seasonal nature of employment, presumably production, high daily wage rates but modest annual
wages, and indifferent profit margin; (2) sweatshops operating mainly with white laborers, with a total labor force of 70
or over and in which the distinctive features were mild seasonal fluctuation, high daily and annual wages, and low or nonexisting investment returns; (3) large Chinese sweatshops (70
workers or over) showing middling seasonality in employment,
low daily and annual earnings for workers and a fair profit;
(4) smaller sweatshops which operated primarily with white
laborers, had a fair income-variable cost ratio, with a low
seasonality in its operation, and modest annual earnings per
worker; (5) the smaller Chinese shops which had a very low
wage rate, a slightly higher seasonality and the highest possible profit margin (of 1,335 Chinese shoe makers, 908, or
over 70 per cent worked in this group); (6) a number of shops
employing one or two laborers, mostly on a seasonal basis
wherein gross annual earnings of the owners were somewhere
between $550 and $750 and net income was at best on par with
the workers in group two, i.e. large white sweatshops; and
(7) a number of Chinese co-operatives under contract to the
wholesalers in which average annual income per worker was a
low $250, and net earnings were perhaps the lowest in the in-
dustry.   The following table demonstrates the above general-
ization.

    From these statistics, another nature of the industry can be
seen as well. The annual earnings of shoe makers in California
were definitely above average in 1880. This was partly due to
the high percentage of high priced boots manufactured. Though
the market was limited, it was free of competition from Eastern
imports and Chinese firms. Thus about 53 per cent of the total
sales in value came from boots for group 2's larger sweatshops,
30 per cent to 37 per cent for group 1's factories, and the white
owners of group 4's smaller shops. None of the Chinese shops
produced any of the boots for men. [33]

TABLE 38

SEASONALITY IN SHOE INDUSTRY IN CALIFORNIA, 1880[34]

	Group				
	1	2	3	4	5
Maximum-average labor force ratio	1.37	1.05	1.28		
Days in operation[a] Maximum limit	285	304	316		
Days in operation[b] Minimum limit	193	280	250		
Daily Wage	$2.25-3.50	$2.00-4.00	$0.75-1.25		
Annual earnings Maximum[c]	$661	$723	$316	$558	$296
Annual earnings Minimum[d]	$483	$688	$253	$504	$248
Gross Income-Variable Cost Ratio	1.22	1.09	1.23	1.21	1.35

[a]Total wage divided by average labor force times average wage rates.
[b]Total wage divided by maximum labor force times average wage rate.
[c]Total wage divided by average labor force.
[d]Total wage divided by maximum labor force.

Some of the larger sweatshops, such as the United Working-men's Boot and Shoe Co., were organized on a co-operative basis with the explicit objective of attaining maximum wages and employment. For this group as a whole, labor costs amounted to 38 per cent of the gross income as compared to 27 per cent to 33 per cent for group 1, and 24 per cent for the Chinese shops. [35]

In summary, figures in the Manuscript Manufacturing Census reveal that the profit situation of shoe shops in California was determined by three major factors—price or the degree of Eastern competition, the wage rate, and the adjustment of production to seasonal sales. The high profit of the small Chinese shops in spite of the low price of their products was due to low wage and a relatively high seasonality in operation. The low, or nonexisting profit of the large white sweatshops was a result of high wage rate and low seasonality, relatively high price of their product and the lack of direct Eastern competition notwithstanding. The fair profit of the shoe factories and large Chinese sweatshops was due to their low wages and high seasonality, though in their field Eastern competition was intense. The moderate profit of the small white sweatshops was the consequence of moderate wage rate, low seasonality, and high price.

Due in part to product specialization, the transition from Chinese labor to white labor had already been accomplished to all intents and purposes in firms owned by white employers in 1880. To my knowledge, there was only one notable exception. One factory still employed 165 Chinese in that year. [36] In no other industry did the disparity of wages between white and Chinese labor even approach that of the shoe industry. Logically, anti-Chinese agitation became senseless thereafter. But it persisted, partly because of inertia, partly because of solidarity among white workers. Actually, the anti-Chinese movement was only part of the battle against the transition from sweatshop to factory, from a labor intensive to a capital intensive mode of production. In this battle, the white workers were certain to be defeated.

Not only did wages between whites and Chinese reveal significant disparities, but those among adult Chinese varied greatly also in 1880, as table 39 shows.

Though the wage scales appear to have been extremely low by comparison with those of the white shoemakers, they were above the average wage paid Chinese workers in other industries.

The Chinese and white sweatshops constituted essentially noncompeting groups, for the former specialized in shoe manufacturing and the latter in boots. In shoe manufacturing, only

TABLE 39

ANNUAL EARNINGS OF CHINESE SHOEMAKERS, 1880[37]

Annual Earnings	Percentage of Workers
$100 or less	4
$200 - $249	30
$250 - $299	34
$300 - $349	27
$350 and up	5

in the $2.00 to $2.49 price range did competition between white and Chinese firms really exist. In this price range two Chinese shops produced $117,716 worth of shoes and eight white firms $214,216. The distribution was as shown in Table 40.

TABLE 40

PRICES OF SHOES BY CHINESE AND WHITE SHOPS, 1880[38]

Price of Shoes Per Pair	Number of Chinese Firms	Number of American Firms
$1.10 - 1.49	33	-
1.50 - 1.99	17	1
2.00 - 2.49	2	8
2.50 and up	1	4

The only Chinese firm which did produce high priced shoes (at $2.60) operated only after April 15, 1880, and turned out 1,008 pairs. The one American firm that manufactured cheap shoes (at $1.50 to $1.99) gained $46,452 in shoes, while its income from boots was $61,200.[39] Otherwise, product differentiation between Chinese and white firms within the shoe industry remained typical. Again, price competition functioned as one of the chief weapons of the Chinese shops. The majority of the Chinese firms, however, did not compete directly with the smaller white shoe manufacturers. On the other hand, where competition between local firms existed, it was primarily between the "factories" and the Chinese sweatshops. Thus the printed census reported that some 81 shoe factories produced 1,006,993 pairs of shoes worth $2,627,941.[40] The average per pair would have been $1.58. In the Manuscript Manufacture Census, two of the leading factories—L. W. Levy & Co., and Buckingham and Hecht respectively produced 60,000 pairs of shoes at $1.70 per pair, and 178,540 at $2.00 per pair.[41] These shoes were obviously priced at a level competitive with the products of the Chinese sweatshops.

In contrast to such competition, slipper manufacturing as an industry in San Francisco was alleged to have fallen exclusively into the hands of the Chinese because of the low capital requirement. A Frenchman founded the first slipper "factory" in San Francisco, but "Every Chinaman whom he employed in turn became a manufacturer... and today the Chinaman has driven France from the field..." someone testified in 1876.[42] The 1870 Manuscript Product of Industry Census recorded 12 slipper "factories," 11 of them owned by Chinese with 182 adult laborers and 9 minors. Only 20 of the adults worked in a firm owned by a white employer. The average capital for these Chinese firms was $1,500 and average earnings per worker about $200. The gross income-variable cost ratio— 1.30.[43] Compared to the shoe industry in the same year, the wage rate was about 33 per cent lower than that of Chinese employed in show factories. The one white firm that had an income-variable cost ratio of 1.14 verged on bankruptcy because of its slightly higher pay rate, $240 annually. Disregarding workers in the Chinese firms which had not operated for a full year, the distribution of wages for adult Chinese slipper makers was as shown in Table 41.

Thus the reason for a Chinese "monopoly" of slipper manufacturing may be found in the character of that low-profit and low-wage industry.

The development of the slipper industry during the 1870's can best be summarized as shown in Table 42. The industry

TABLE 41

EARNINGS OF CHINESE SLIPPER WORKERS, 1870[44]

Annual Earnings Per Worker	Number of Workers
$199 or less	76
200 - 249	65
250 or up	17

reached its peak of product value per worker in 1875-1876, in total value of product in 1876-1878, and in employment in 1878-1881. There was considerable under-employment after 1876, especially after 1878. It can be argued with great plausibility

TABLE 42

SLIPPER INDUSTRY IN SAN FRANCISCO, 1869-1881[45]

Year	Number of Firms	Number of Workers	Value of Product	Value of Product Per Worker
1869-1870	6	90	$ 60,000	666
1870-1871	9	125	100,000	800
1871-1872		Data not available		
1872-1873				
1873-1874	28	213	162,000	760
1874-1875	18	300	200,000	666
1875-1876	18	370	310,000	837
1876-1877	18	750	500,000	666
1877-1878	18	750	500,000	666
1878-1879	25	1,000	470,000	470
1879-1880	25	1,000	470,000	470
1880-1881	25	1,000	470,000	470

that slipper manufacturing was typically a sick industry, with only occasionally prosperous years between 1870 and 1874 and in the 1875-1876 season. This was undoubtedly the precise reason why it was left for the Chinese.

The 1880 Manuscript Manufacture Census contained a partial list of slipper "factories" and co-operatives. Average earnings per worker in the former approximated $256 and that of the latter $251. Both registered a gain from the 1870 level. The income-variable cost ratio for the shops which stood at a low 1.19, revealed that these shops were in a very precarious financial situation. [46]

The difficulties of shoe factories in the 1880's were, however, not entirely due either to high labor costs or a technical lag.[47] Factories in California, woolen included, were plagued by high overhead in the postwar deflationary period. When prices fell, overhead formed a higher percentage of the selling price and tended to be fixed in money terms. The profit margin was cut. Overhead costs in California were often exceptionally high due to high borrowing charges, high transportation costs for machinery, and high construction costs. This high over-head put California factories in a disadvantageous competitive position and exercised a strong downward pressure upon wages and employment. In focusing their attention on variable costs, especially wages, the effect of fixed cost tended to be ignored.

In summary, shoe manufacturing in California was, perhaps, one of the fortunate industries. Product specialization was feasible to a degree that minimized competition with Eastern imports. In other industries, as in cigar making, the absence of such leeway proved of crucial importance.

Part II: Cigar and Fringe Industries

Actually the very first attempt to introduce Chinese labor into manufacturing had occurred in the cigar industry. The Segar (cigar) Makers' association in November, 1859, passed a resolution in opposition to such action. The union fought a forlorn battle without either allies or the endorsement of public opinion. The arguments so forceful in winning public support

and so effective in obtaining legislative action for the miners
in 1852, fell upon unsympathetic ears. The time was inoppor-
tune. Anti-Chinese sentiment had spent its force in the mines
and the exodus of independent miners had already begun. Chinese mining laborers were employed "extensively" and on the
whole were ignored by the public and tolerated by other miners
in the 1850's and early 1860's.   Therefore, since the number
of cigar makers was minute, it did seem far-fetched to identify
the interests of this small group of workers with the interests
of the state, the welfare of the people and the destiny of the
nation.   Indeed, the San Francisco Bulletin in one of its editorials commented:[1]

> I cannot, however, for the life of me, see how the
> employment of the Chinese in the making of segars can
> be considered "as destroying the true basis of our
> country's prosperity," or likely to "bring want and suf-
> fering into the homes of our people;" nor can I see how
> "it will prove destructive to the general welfare, and
> retard the advancement of civilization and the manifest
> destiny of our country:" nor how "it will inflict a deadly
> injury on our dearest rights."

However, the alarm of the cigar makers was premature. As
white miners left their claims, the Chinese raced for the mines.
Not until after 1863 were Chinese available as industrial wage
laborers in any quantity.

The first period of expansion in the cigar industry occurred
from 1864 to 1866. As the 1867 San Francisco Directory indicated, the total value of cigars manufactured in the city
jumped from $2,000 in the former year to $1,000,000 in the
latter.[2]   Precisely at this time the Chinese first entered into
cigar making; thus the Alta California reported in 1867 that out
of the 500 employed in the industry only 50 were white.[3]

Another major stimulus for the growth of the cigar industry
in California was the Civil War, which disrupted regular import,
as Table 43 indicates. When the War ended, cigar manufacturing on the Coast had already become well established, and
by 1868, California replaced Massachusetts as the fourth
largest cigar-producing state.[4]

TABLE 43

CIGAR IMPORTS, 1860-1869[5]

Year	Cases Imported
1860	6, 569
1861	3, 504
1862	2, 779
1864	2, 374
1865	1, 861
1866	1, 740
1867	733
1869	678

Further data on the manufacturing of cigars contained in the annual San Francisco Municipal Reports is shown in Table 44.

TABLE 44

CIGAR MANUFACTURING IN SAN FRANCISCO, 1867-1881[6]

Year	Number of Firms	Number of Workers	Number of Cigars Produced	Monthly Capacity
1867-1868	60	1, 132	35, 672, 000	3, 000, 000
1868-1869			38, 692, 000	3, 500, 000
1869-1870	63	1, 597	38, 414, 000	4, 152, 000
1870-1871	151	2, 500	60, 000, 000 ($ 1, 500, 000)	
1871-1872			50, 000, 000	
1872-1873			55, 400, 000	No. of cigarettes
1873-1874	115	data incomplete		produced
1874-1875	120	4, 000	95, 000, 000	
1875-1876	251	3, 000	113, 000, 000	7, 000, 000
1876-1877	200	4, 000	107, 000, 000	7, 000, 000
1877-1878	200	4, 000	107, 000, 000	7, 000, 000
1878-1879	200	4, 000	107, 000, 000	7, 000, 000
1879-1880	200	3, 200	82, 000, 000	9, 000, 000
1880-1881	200	3, 500	91, 000, 000	9, 900, 000

From 1867 to 1869 production of cigars in San Francisco proceeded at full capacity level, but a mild recession occurred in 1869-1870. In 1871-1872, capacity (judging from the number of firms and workers employed) increased faster than production. Recession set in again in 1871-1873. Then once again expansion of capacity outstripped production in the 1874-1875 season. The peak year was 1875-1876. Reduction of production during 1876-1877 led to considerable under-employment. Recovery began some time later in 1880 and 1881, but except for the years 1867-1869 and 1875-1876, production was far below capacity and under-employment was probable.

The employment of Chinese in cigar manufacturing, as in other industries, stemmed from the scarcity of labor. According to Willis Baer, there were only 4,000 cigar markers in the United States in 1865. [7] In addition, the cigar makers' union which was struggling to survive, repeatedly attempted to enforce a three-year apprenticeship. [8] This further limited the source of labor supply. The first Chinese cigar makers in San Francisco were very likely ex-miners. During 1865-1867, when the cigar industry in California rose from near nonexistence to a position of one of the leading producers in the United States, departures for China exceeded new arrivals of Chinese immigrants in San Francisco.

The entry of Chinese labor into cigar making preceded the discharge of laborers by the Central Pacific in 1869. As in the case of the clothing industry, when entry was easy, it was notoriously common for Chinese workers to set up their own shops soon after they learned the trade. As early as 1866, half of the cigar "factories" were owned by the Chinese. [9] In 1870 there were 1,881 cigar makers in San Francisco, of whom 1,667 were Chinese. In the state as a whole, 1,705 out of 1,902 were of the same racial origin. [10] In both cases the Chinese made up more than 90 per cent of the total labor force.

Among the 16 Chinese cigar "factories" listed in the 1870 Manuscript Product of Industry Census, twelve used Spanish names, a practice they kept for the next two decades. Four hundred and nine adult workers and twelve minors were employed in these shops. The average annual earnings was about $236.

TABLE 45

ANNUAL EARNINGS OF CHINESE
IN CHINESE CIGAR SHOPS, 1870[11]

Number of Workers	Annual Earnings
78	$300 or over
140	250 - 299
189	249 or less

The dispersion was as shown above.

The average gross income-variable cost ratio for these Chinese firms was 1.51. Therefore profit margin was quite high, but wages were low. The gross income-variable cost ratio for firms owned by white employers was lower, probably because of higher labor costs. The following figures further elaborate this.

TABLE 46

ANNUAL EARNINGS OF CIGAR MAKERS
IN WHITE CIGAR FACTORIES, 1870[11]

Number of Workers	Annual Earnings
279	$400 and over
219	300 - 399
115	250 - 299
340	249 or less

Cigar manufacturing, in fact, was notorious for ease of entry. Two Chinese firms reported a capital of $300 each, and quite a few white firms had a capital as low as $500 each in 1870. [13] Among the 200 cigar shops in San Francisco during the second half of the 1870's, between 70 to 90 were owned by Chinese. Only 23 to 28 of the latter reported a capitalization of $1,000 or above in city tax assessments or in the Manuscript Manufacture Census. [14]

The extent of seasonal employment was revealed by the differences between maximum labor force and average labor force. As reported in the Manuscript Manufacture Census of 1880, only the large firms conformed with general seasonal patterns of the nation. Shops with 25 or less workers reported a fairly stable labor force throughout the year. If this was the case, there must have been a great deal of under-employment in these shops. The majority of firms owned by white proprietors were operating at full capacity only 160 days for the census year of 1880. [15]

Seasonal fluctuations of Chinese firms seem to have been less pronounced, exclusive of the co-operatives. [16]

TABLE 47

SEASONALITY IN CHINESE CIGAR SHOPS, 1880

Working Days in a Year	Number of Firms
200 - 300	20
300 and up	16

The differences in seasonal employment between firms owned by Chinese and whites was also demonstrated in the disparity of annual earnings. This disparity was much more moderate than between respective daily wage rates. White employers paid between $1.25 to $2.00 for adult cigar makers, and $0.50 to $1.25 for minors. The Chinese had a much lower wage of $0.65 to $1.75 for adults, and $0.40 to $0.90 for minors. Annual earnings of employees in shops owned by white employers was about $250.[17] Wage distribution of laborers in Chinese firms were as shown in Table 48. [18]

Since the average gross income-variable cost ratio for the Chinese firms was 1.18,[19] they were on the brink of bankruptcy, despite the comparative low wage rate. The shops owned by white employers stood at 1.36, partly because of the high earnings of a few firms with a labor force of more than 100 each.

TABLE 48

WAGE RATES OF CHINESE CIGAR SHOPS, 1880

Annual Earnings	Number of Workers
$400 or up	75
300 - 399	87
250 - 299	281
200 - 249	280
200 or less	245

The ratio for the industry as a whole was 1.3 and wages were at $240.[20] These large firms were characterized by the moderate pay rate of $1.20 to $1.75 for adults, and $0.75 to $1.25 for minors. Seasonality was high; the maximum labor force was as high as 182 per cent of its average labor force for one firm. Investment returns were also high. The gross income-variable cost ratio was above 1.90.[21]

There was a divergent movement of profit margins between large and small manufacturers. While the investment return of the former improved between 1870 and 1880, that of the latter deteriorated. This was partially explained by the inability of the smaller firms to adjust production and hence labor cost to seasonal or random variations of sales. But, perhaps more important, the firms in California were not competing with the average firm in New York but with more efficient ones producing for a national market.

The low profit margin of the smaller cigar shops in California was undoubtedly a primary reason for the tenuous alliance between cigar makers and small employers. The former would benefit most if Chinese labor could be expelled, if not in wages certainly in employment.[22] But that would have bankrupted the small sweatshop owners whose primary objective was the elimination of Chinese cigar shops and the retention or even the enlargement of their own Chinese labor force.

After a determined and vigorous campaign against the Chinese had been waged in the early 1880's, the cigar makers' union finally succeeded in virtual elimination of Chinese labor and Chinese sweatshops in cigar manufacturing. The industry itself suffered a marked decline.

TABLE 49

RECEIPTS OF CIGAR STAMPS SOLD AT SAN FRANCISCO
1881-1883[23]

Year	Receipts
1881	$12, 430. 91
1882	7, 021. 31
1883	2, 519. 75

Wage and employment conditions of white workers improved very little. Capital stayed away because of high investment returns in other fields. In 1880, of the 3, 217 cigar makers in California, 2, 757 were Chinese, and 2, 717 were in San Francisco alone. By the mid-1880's only a few hundred remained. [24] Chinese cigar makers were among the first to make the transition from a manufacturing industry to a service industry.

Aside from the four major manufacturing industries—woolen, clothing, shoe and cigar—numerous Chinese were employed also in such manufacturers as soap, candles, watches, brushes, brooms, glues, bricks and powder. Their wage scale was comparable to those in other manufacturing industries—$1. 00 to $1. 25 between 1870 and 1880. Low wages and seasonal employment in the bag, canned fruits, pickle "factories," flour and lumber mills made the employment of Chinese a common place.

About 2,899 Chinese were employed in laundries, and 4, 315 as domestic servants in 1870.[25] There were 5, 435 laundrymen, and 7, 825 servants in 1880,[26] primarily as a result of the disparity in the sex ratio in California's population. There were also 1,193 Chinese fishermen in 1880.[27] They engaged mainly in shrimp and abalone fishing, serving the demand of the Chinese community in California and exporting a large portion of dry

shrimps and abalones to China.[28] Chinese peddlers who brought
vegetables, fruits, fish and sundry merchandise to the door
steps of consumers numbered 1,248 in 1880.[29] They were mainly
distributors of the wholesalers.

A number of gambling houses in the various Chinatowns and
prostitutes in major cities served to satisfy the diversionary
and glandular needs of the male laborers. Chinese country
storekeepers, artisans, jewelers, carpenters, coopers, tinners,
and professionals such as physicians serving the Chinese communities are beyond the scope of this study.

Finally we have to examine the nature of Chinese labor contracts. It is one of the most obscure points in history. The
widespread reports of exploitation at the time were no doubt
based on hearsay evidence. These accounts were used as additional arguments for the expulsion of the Chinese. As a de-
fensive measure, details of such contracts were the best
guarded secrets within the Chinese community at the time, and
later buried with the contractual parties.[30]

One of the most reliable reports on such activities was, perhaps, an interview given to the San Francisco Chronicle in
1876. According to the informant, the contractors charged the
laborers a flat fee or a commission of 50 cents per person, and
furnished the transportation facilities if necessary. In return
the contractor gained the right to board the crew at $8 to $10
per person per month, and provided one cook for every 25 persons. Capital was usually borrowed from Chinese merchants.[31]
The figure of $10 per month for board seemed to be too low, as
Chinese country storekeepers charged $15 or more. The larger
contractors seem to have been white. Sisson, Wallace & Co.
was the main supplier of Chinese laborers to the Central Pacific
Railroad.[32] The Pacific Chinese Employment Co. , King & Merritt
proprietors, claimed in advertisements in the interior towns to
have special arrangements with " principle Chinese companies."
They asserted that they were better prepared to send out laborers of all kinds, from one to thousands, at a shorter notice
than any competitor on the Coast.[33] The advertisement was
discontinued in 1877.

Because of the inadequacies of the San Francisco Labor Exchange many large employers undoubtedly relied upon the

services of such contractors or employment agencies. The 1880 manuscript population census listed five officers and five employees of two Chinese agencies. The scope of operation is unknown; however, many employers often obtained additional Chinese labor simply by asking a Chinese employee.

CHAPTER VII

CONFLICTING VIEWS ON THE EFFECTS
OF CHINESE IMMIGRATION ON CALIFORNIA'S ECONOMY

In the course of history major economic dislocations have induced vigorous inquiry and searching reexamination of the adequacies of the prevailing political economy. California's economy in the 1870's typified one such period. Material pertaining to the debate on the political economy of California has already reached seemingly unmanageable proportions. However, the repetitious nature of much evidence permits concentration upon certain basic issues. Each of these in the context of California history was intricately tied in with the Chinese problem.

One of the major issues was the controversy between the employer and the workers. This centered upon the proper limits of property ownership. Did ownership imply the absolute freedom of management? What were, if any, the responsibilities of the employer to his employee? Was his responsibility only the fulfillment of his lawful contracts? Had the employer a moral obligation to substitute white laborers for Chinese, at least during periods of widespread unemployment?

A related, if lesser, field of contention pertained to the proper role of government—national, state, and local—in economic affairs. Was the alleviation of economic distress a proper function of the government? Did widespread unemployment merit governmental concern and action; and, what was the boundary of authority of the respective levels of government in this issue?

The employers, on the whole, argued these issues along the line of pure laissez-faire economics. They learned to their distress and even despair that economics became

129

increasingly a matter of politics and ethics as the depression spread. This proved especially true when the Chinese problem was injected into the great debate on political economy. For instance, witnesses appearing before an 1876 Congressional Joint Special Committee to Investigate Chinese Immigration were repeatedly asked to exclude from their minds "all the facts and all the arguments tending to show the material advancement of the state under Chinese labor, and consider the moral and the political welfare" of the country.[1]

In the field of ethics, few employers were prepared to take a stand on racial equality, or to denounce discrimination as contrary to Christian ethics and the American sense of justice. Rather, they stressed the feasibility of substituting white for Chinese labor and dwelt at length on the scarcity of labor in California. The employers usually denied that an army of unemployed was ready and eager to take over any openings made by the dismissal of Chinese. The requirements for employment, they pointed out, were certain specific skills at a certain wage, and not mere willingness to be employed.[2] This argument was weighty, and its propriety may be freely conceded with certain minor reservations. Nevertheless, it was not entirely persuasive to the California community during a period of depression.

The employers also put forward the contention that commodity price determined input and factor price. Thus the levels of wage and employment were set by commodity price over which California manufacturers had no influence.[3] They further maintained that the process of equalization of wage levels throughout the United States, or even the world, was inevitable.[4] They argued that the current widespread unemployment was both result and proof of unusually high wage rates prevalent in the state.[5] Were the substitution of white labor for Chinese put into effect, they held, subsequent wage and price increases for goods manufactured locally would result in the immediate bankruptcy of many firms and industries. A decline in certain sectors of the economy would inescapably reduce profitability and employment in other fields; it would also further accelerate the downswing of business. In effect, the employers took every opportunity to assert the potential cumulative bad effects of expulsion of Chinese on profit, employment, and the general well being of the state.[6]

The substantial accuracy of this reasoning is not open to serious doubt. The total effect of a single factor, such as low wages, on the economy as a whole, however, is at best difficult to assess. No allowance was made for the fact that wages were not the only cause of economic difficulties in California. Outdated machinery and obsolete business organizations were at least of equal importance but received scant attention. In the cigar, clothing and related industries, inefficient sweatshops could not long survive even with Chinese labor. That too was largely ignored.

It was, of course, very difficult to secure popular acceptance of laissez-faire arguments during a depression. Doing something, anything at all, seemed infinitely better than doing nothing. Moreover, the public appears to have been totally unimpressed with the dire consequences that might accompany any substitution for Chinese labor. Impending doom was on the horizon anyway.

The employers argued repeatedly that the employment of Chinese labor in certain industries had not replaced white workers but had in reality induced expansion and growth in many other industries and thereby created new jobs for white workers.[7] They stressed the idea that the increase in wealth resulting from employment of Chinese would benefit the community far more than any alternative.[8] Few went so far as to pronounce publicly, as did Augustus Layres, that cheap labor is the creator of capital and real source of wealth.[9] An obvious defect in this logic as a means of persuasion exists. The beneficial effects were indirect; they were not clearly demonstrable in prosperity and seemed far-fetched, if not downright absurd, in a depression.

Some employers were of the opinion that widespread unemployment was not so much the consequence of surplus labor as of scarcity of capital. Labor had to be accompanied by capital; given the latter, full employment would follow without benefit of any social action.[10] In other words, such men stressed the causal relationship between under-investment and depression and its attendant effect of unemployment. Low wage as an inducement to investment was essential to prosperity and to the full utilization of human resources. Argument along this line has merit only when other conditions remain equal between California and the East.   Granted that plant modern-ization was a precondition for improving the competitive posi-tion of manufacturing industries of California; a low wage alone could never furnish sufficient incentive for new invest-ment in California.   Other factors such as the size of market, raw material supply, credit facilities, etc. , were not favorable during the 1870's.

Another favorable argument of the employers was that low wages raised real income by lowering prices, stimulating con-sumption, accelerating economic growth in prosperity, and hastening recovery during a recession. [11] However, the appli-cability of this logic to the particular circumstances in Cali-fornia in the 1870's was dubious at best.   As price levels in general were determined by Eastern imports, the relationship between local wages and price levels, except in service in-dustries, was not a significant one.   It would have taken an immense influx of cheap labor, as well as capital investment in modern machinery, to have had any noticeable effect on price or to have set off a chain reaction tending toward recovery.

In opposition to the employers' laissez-faire economics, the workers based their arguments upon primacy of the human rights of the white workers.   They contended that a delay in realizing the maximum rate of economic growth was a small price to pay for immediate mitigation of unemployment.   The welfare of the individual, especially the white worker, should take precedent over profit. When confronted with the alterna-tives of the possible economic consequence of the expulsion of the Chinese and extensive unemployment among the white community, employers and society itself were held to be mor-ally obligated to the full employment of the white workers. [12] Moreover, the resultant lower rate of growth of white labor was regarded as desirable since it would lead to a more equitable distribution of income. [13]

In answering the employers, the workers further asserted that the substitution of white for Chinese labor would expand money income in the market to take up the slack in business. They reasoned that consumption on the part of the white workers was only limited by their wage and employment opportunities. [14] In contrast, they claimed that Chinese consumption was primarily determined by a low standard of living, which was not subject to change in the conceivable future. Since the Chinese subsisted on a sub-starvation level, mostly on imports from China, their annual remittance was considered to be a serious drain on California's economy. [15] Furthermore, by reducing wage rates, the Chinese were said to have also reduced the white workers' spending power and thus to have caused a depression. [16]

This reasoning could have had an element of truth only when the increases in the workers' earning power and propensity to consume were of such a magnitude that they induced a strong upward trend in the price level of the United States as a whole, which in turn would have stimulated manufacturing in the state. Short of that, the employers' contention was the correct one. The immediate consequences of a wage raise could have been only a narrowing of profit margins for some firms, bankruptcy for others, and a consequent increase in unemployment.

In reply to the employers' insistence that commodity price be the sole determinant of factor price and input, the workers responded with the theory that input and factor price or wages were determined by their supply. To the workers, the deplorable situation of the 1870's was due entirely to the competition of the Chinese. So long as this alien labor force was in existence, the employment opportunity of white workers was chronically jeopardized. Hence the most effective means of achieving a living wage was exclusion of the alien labor reserve. [17]

Increasing the scarcity value of labor through restriction of its supply merited consideration only in a period of economic expansion. In a recession the relationship between scarcity and price was quite removed. Even granting that Chinese labor depressed wage levels, no satisfactory evidence exists to maintain that this exclusion would have resulted in a wage increase during a business downswing. The workers had ignored demand for labor entirely.

In refuting the employers' contention that low wages increased real earning through a reduction of price, the workers maintained that the low wages of the Chinese never reduced price but only enhanced profit.[18] On the whole, the statement that Chinese labor had little or no effect on general price level is accurate. However, because of Eastern competition few manufacturing industries in California in the years 1870 to 1880 were able to achieve huge investment returns. Even the profits of San Francisco's woolen mills and shoe factories are seen to have been quite modest when compared to interest rate. Probably the immense fortune of the Central Pacific Railroad was the only notable exception. The employment of Chinese could conceivably have saved several million dollars in wages. However, at that time white labor was not available in large quantities; therefore the question was more or less academic.

Moreover, the workers' faith in the efficacy of solving the unemployment problem through increasing the scarcity value of labor by exclusion of Chinese was in part due to a misconception of early California history. To the casual observer, high wages had been responsible for the unusually high prices in early California, and the scarcity of labor had been the primary reason for high wages. However, wage rates in early California were determined by interactions between the incomes of the independent miners and the degree of Eastern competition through commodity import. Thus, the wages of shoemakers and tailors had always been low and scarcity had little effect on their wage scale.

Another difficulty was involved in the campaign for substitution of white workers for the Chinese. This was the predominant position of Chinese sweatshops in certain industries. In the latter small manufactures and workers joined forces. The Chinese had been charged with "monopolizing" certain industries to the exclusion of white workers and manufacturers. The fact was that the term "monopoly," a symbol of economic injustice during the turbulent agrarian and industrial revolts, was transferred to an entirely different situation. This is another example of the close tie between the anti-Chinese and anti-capitalist movements.

Moreover, the "monopolistic" position of Chinese firms in clothing, shoe and cigar manufacturing was partially a by-product of the anti-Chinese movement itself. After being

discharged from factories and sweatshops, the Chinese workers often set up their own shops in these trades. Thus the
close relationship between mass discharge of Chinese workers
in 1876 and the increase of Chinese sweatshops can be illustrated by the following table: [19]

TABLE 50

NUMBER OF CHINESE FIRMS IN
CIGAR, CLOTHING AND SHOE MANUFACTURING, 1876-1877

Industry	1876	1877
Cigar	88	120
Clothing	21	51
Shoe	43	61

Furthermore, no evidence has been found that Chinese manufacturers acted in collusion to restrict supply or to influence
price during this period. They were highly competitive among
themselves. The two factors which prevented white manufacturers and laborers from entering into or hastening the exit of
the whites from such trades as cigar, slipper, overalls or
women's underwear were low wages and low profit margins.
These were the result of pure competition, the antithesis of
monopoly. Nevertheless, workers and small entrepreneurs
alike believed that the elimination of Chinese sweatshops in
their respective field would raise prices, profits, wages and
the employment level.

The vital flaw in this line of reasoning can be readily discerned. By the mid-1870's Chinese and white-owned and operated sweatshops were no longer competing directly. In the
shoe, clothing and related industries the latter were found
mostly in custom-made trades. These aimed at a high value
per unit of output, used more expensive materials and sometimes much labor per unit of output. The products of the Chinese firms were often competing with factory-made goods, as
in the ready-made trade. The basic problem in the custom
trade was the diminishing share in the total market as a higher

output per worker and lower price per unit mode of factory production reached maturity. The loss of sales was further accen-
tuated, as might have been expected, by the protracted
depression of the 1870's.

Most of the sweatshops had reached a point where further
technological advancement beyond their current stage would
require an entirely new productive method and organizational
form—that of the factory. That capital requirement, however,
was out of the reach of nearly all the shopowners. Not every
small entrepreneur was endowed with the necessary managerial
ability. Industrialization had passed them by and they were
unable to share the benefit of an expanding mass market. After
the advent of industrialization, entry to the quality custom
trade also demanded considerable capital, promotional skill
and organizational talent. Sweatshops were the victims of the
process of economic change. The elimination of those owned
by one race could hardly have reversed the trend.

Technological changes led as well to a hierarchy of profits.
Large capital was concentrated in trades enjoying a high rate
of investment returns, as in railroads and factory manufacturing. Small capital was crowded into fields where profit was
low and diminishing. Caught in this process, apprehensive
over the loss of their status as independent producers, lacking
any understanding of the workings of "economic forces," small
manufacturers of cigars, shoes, and clothing rose to vent their
anger upon a scapegoat as had the independent miners in the
1850's.

Then anti-Chinese agitations which were directed against
independent Chinese miners had obtained sympathetic legislation. The effectiveness of such legislations was at best dubious, but there had been no uncertainty as to the objectives of
such acts nor hesitance as to the necessity and propriety of
government action.

During the urban anti-Chinese agitation, however, the
small manufacturers and the workers could not agree upon appropriate and necessary legislation. They were unsure of the
proper limit of government action and intervention and were at
a loss as to the desired limit upon local, state and federal
authority. They would agree on only one issue—desire for the

exclusion of Chinese, and this, they finally conceded, was under federal authority. Divergence of interests between the workers and the small sweatshop owners made any common front tenuous from the very beginning.

However, all employers and labor were unalterably committed to the intrinsic truth of automatic prosperity and full employment. The truism that under the American system depression and unemployment were only transitory deviations from the norm of prosperity and full employment was held to be self-evident. It required no positive proof in the minds of Californians in the 1870's. Only the cause of these temporary aberrations was a subject of debate and contention. To the majority of employers, the widespread business failures and unemployment in California were definite proof that local wage rates were too high. It was the firm belief of the workers and the small manufacturers in the clothing, cigar and shoe industries that Chinese competition was the sole cause of such economic imbalance. Because of this unfailing belief in automatic prosperity and full employment, no fundamental changes in the economy were contemplated. Even the question of how the expulsion of Chinese could be best adapted to serve the imperative objectives of a living wage for labor and a fair profit for small capital was begged in the great debate. [20]

Moreover, in the overall anti-Chinese movement, neither the small manufacturers nor the industrial workers could exercise a decisive influence in its direction. Because of their numerical superiority in San Francisco, Irish nonindustrial labor had taken over the leadership, personified by the rise of Denis Kearney. Kearney's major contributions to the movement were his personality and the slogan, "the Chinese must go." Characteristically, his own Draymen and Teamsters' Union was singularly immune against Chinese competition. His personality, however, caught the imagination of workers in California. Slogans focused upon the single issue wherein skilled and unskilled workers, small businessmen, some farmers and the politicians could form a common front. They also served well to disarm the employers. Unwilling to defend the rights of all men, including Chinese, the employer had to resort to arguments of economic necessity and economic growth;

neither of these was an effective vote-getter.

The multiplicity of factors in the business recession had no necessary and compelling interest to the public as a whole. Thus the Chinese served as a convenient personification for the obscure forces which caused the business and employment situation to be different from expectation. The Chinese became a suitable target in lieu of impersonal forces of depression. Furthermore, there was a cultural and racial solidarity among the whites. Some employers had a vague sense of guilt for employing Chinese while white men were suffering. Many had conceded the primacy of achieving an equality of opportunity among the in-group by denying it to the Chinese—the out-group. By and large, then, the technique of anti-Chinese agitation proved effective. Sandlot meetings served the dual purpose of crystallizing the objective and fixing a definite target.

As the anti-Chinese movement gained momentum, the prime objective, means of restoring or achieving an equitable economic opportunity and reward for all Caucasians, was pushed to the background. It was soon completely forgotten. The means, the expulsion of the Chinese, became all important. At the same time, preoccupation with the Chinese issue on the part of the workers precluded any effective farmer-worker alliance.

With intensive agitation but no specific program, the bewildered workers resorted to mob violence as depression persisted. When law and order were seriously threatened, employers' resistance stiffened. Small businessmen shifted back to the rank of property owners; and the farmers, alarmed by the spread of disorder in rural areas, took over the control of the 1878-1879 Constitutional Convention. Thus, a second realignment of power took place. The workers were isolated and their claim to economic opportunity and reward denied. Three years later the Chinese Exclusion Act passed Congress.

APPENDIX I

Prices for Staples, 1851-1856

	Beef per bbl. $	Pork per bbl. $	Flour per 200 lb. $	Rice Chinese per lb. Cts.	Beans Chili per lb. Cts.
Jan. 1851	15-16	14-17	17-15	4-6	6-5
July	12-16	14-15	9-11	5	3-4½
Jan. 1852	10-12	10-12	11	2-3	2-3
May	30-25	20-33	7 - 9	5	4-½
Sept.	16-17	35-48	32-30	30	10
Dec.	16-17	45-35	41-30	12½ -15	5-4
May 1853	25-28	28-21½	9½-10½	4-3	5½-7½
Aug.	25-16½	28-24	19-18	4½-7½	5
Jan. 1854	15-12½	16½	10½-10	6-4½	7½-5½
March	11-16	19	7 - 9	4½-4	6½-5½
May	18-22	26	9¼- 8¼	6-6½	7-6½
Sept.	11-12	16½	7½-7¼	5-4½	6-7
Jan. 1855	23-16	19	9-11	10- 8	6
May	14-15½	17	5½- 6	5- 7	7-5½
Oct.	22-24	38	9½- 9	9- 7	8-8¼
June 1856	16	24	9½-10½	7- 8	6¼
Dec.	16	37	7	6¾	--

(Appendix I, continued) — Price for Staples, 1851-1856[*]

	Coffee Manilla per lb. Cts.	Sugar Manilla per lb. Cts.	Dried Apples per lb. Cts.	Coal Anthracite per ton $
Jan. 1851	14-16	6-8	8-12	14-15
July	12-13	4-5	7½-5	10-11
Jan. 1852	9-11	4-5½	4-5½	30-32
May	13-13½	9-10	9	42-35
Sept.	20-21	8-8½	10	40
Dec.	20½-19	6	10-10½	19-22
May 1853	11½	6½-7	9½	13-18
Aug.	16-14½	10-11	10-10½	24
Jan. 1854	20-11½	9-7½	9-6	32-28
March	14-13½	7¼-8	6¼-8	26-25
May	13½	8¼-9½	11-10	30-40
Sept.	18	8¼-8½	9½-10¼	21-32
Jan. 1855	14	10-11	11	21-18
May	14-13	8¼-8¼	9¼-8½	15-19
Oct.	18	9-9¼	20-24	25½-19
June 1856	13½	8½	10	19-20
Dec.	13½	8	12-12½	16

---

[*]H. H. Bancroft, <u>History of California</u>, VII, 111.

APPENDIX II

California Gold Production

Year	Annual gold production estimates by L. A. Garnett
1848	$ 245, 301
1849	10, 151, 306
1850	41, 273, 106
1851	75, 983, 232
1852	81, 294, 700
1853	67, 613, 487
1854	69, 433, 931
1855	55, 485, 396
1856	57, 509, 411
1857	43, 628, 172
1858	46, 591, 140
1859	45, 846, 599
1860	44, 095, 163
1861	41, 884, 995
1862	48, 854, 688
1863	23, 501, 736
1864	24, 071, 423
1865	17, 930, 858
1866	17, 123, 867
1867	18, 265, 452
1868	17, 555, 867
1869	18, 229, 040
1870	17, 458, 133
1871	17, 477, 885
1872	15, 482, 194
1873	15, 019, 210
1874	17, 264, 836
1875	16, 876, 009
1876	15, 610, 723
1877	16, 601, 268
1878	18, 839, 141
1879	18, 839, 141
1880	20, 030, 761

Second Report of the State Minerologist of California, Dec.
1880-Oct. 1882 (Sacramento, 1882), 171.

APPENDIX III

Chinese Immigration

Year	Arrivals	Departures	Net
1849	325		
1850	450		
1851	2,716		
1852	20,026	1,768	18,258
1853	4,270	4,421	- 151
1854	16,084	2,339	13,745
1855	3,329	3,473	- 144
1856	4,807	3,028	1,779
1857	5,924	1,932	3,992
1858	5,427	2,542	2,885
1859	3,175	2,450	725
1860	7,343	2,088	5,255
1861	8,434	3,594	4,840
1862	8,188	2,795	5,393
1863	6,435	2,947	3,488
1864	2,696	3,911	- 1,215
1865	3,097	2,298	799
1866	2,242	3,113	- 871
1867	4,794	4,999	- 205
1868	11,085	4,209	6,876
1869	14,994	4,896	10,098
1870	10,869	4,232	6,637
1871	5,542	3,264	2,278
1872	9,773	4,887	4,886
1873	17,075	6,805	10,270
1874	16,085	7,710	8,375
1875	18,021	6,305	11,716
1876	22,781	8,525	14,256
1877	10,594	8,161	2,433
1878	8,992	8,168	806
1879	9,604	9,220	384
1880	5,802	7,496	- 1,694

Mary Robert Coolidge, Chinese Immigration (New York, 1909), 498.

APPENDIX IV

Imports and exports from San Francisco

Year	Merchandise	Treasure	Imports
1848-50	$ 2,000,000	$66,000,000	
1851	1,000,000	45,989,000	
1852	1,500,000	45,779,000	
1853	2,000,000	54,965,000	
1854	2,500,000	52,045,633	
1855	4,189,611	45,161,731	5,951,379
1856	4,270,516	50,697,434	7,298,837
1857	4,369,758	48,976,692	9,137,414
1858	4,770,163	47,548,826	8,989,733
1859	5,533,411	47,640,462	11,163,558
1860	8,532,439	42,325,916	9,580,868
1861	9,888,072	40,676,785	8,506,506
1862	10,565,294	42,561,761	8,189,908
1863	13,877,399	46,071,920	10,682,409
1864	13,271,752	50,707,201	15,065,478
1865	14,554,130	44,426,172	
1866	17,281,848	44,365,688	
1867	22,421,298	40,671,797	
1868	22,844,235	36,358,096	19,503,980
1869	20,846,349	37,287,114	18,088,901
1870	17,769,742	32,983,139	27,534,402
1871	13,992,283	17,243,340	20,384,907
1872	23,698,598	29,330,433	33,330,501

San Francisco _Bulletin_, Jan. 7, 1873. (Figures from _Annual report and statements of Chief of the Bureau of Statistics on Commerce and Navigation_, put out by the Treasure Department show some slight variations.

APPENDIX V

Data on Selected Manufacturing Industries

States	No. of Firms	Number of Employees				Capital	Wage	Material	Value of Product
		Total	Male	Female	Youth				
Textile Industry 1870									
Cal.	6	663	588	31	44	$ 1,786,000	$ 232,600	$ 609,184	$ 1,107,854
Mass.	427	72,464	27,256	36,409	8,799	72,548,475	23,656,614	71,619,650	112,763,211
N.Y.	422	21,969	8,977	9,238	3,754	23,137,703	7,023,374	19,151,712	31,473,172
Boot and Shoe 1870									
Cal.	420	1,526	1,387	112	27	489,854	629,873	966,952	2,214,807
Mass.	2,392	54,831	42,522	11,193	1,116	19,559,738	27,265,283	51,363,406	88,399,583
N.Y.	3,024	17,501	14,158	2,192	1,151	6,855,657	6,215,063	10,692,075	22,679,874
Tobacco 1870									
Cal.	91	1,858	1,805	4	49	709,345	534,775	807,081	1,967,717
Mass.	136	1,050	784	250	16	507,885	454,884	737,483	1,670,932
N.Y.	1,123	10,243	6,628	2,064	1,551	6,226,040	3,750,870	9,763,626	18,940,658
Men's Clothing 1870									
Cal.	108	528	362	161	5	117,504	295,232	470,102	1,090,270
Mass.	446	9,878	3,031	6,730	117	5,090,764	3,815,742	11,913,317	20,212,407
N.Y.	1,541	28,793	12,367	16,231	195	14,782,043	8,826,008	27,982,394	46,375,369
Women's Clothing 1870									
Cal.	69	229	44	185	-	174,378	84,260	514,350	738,339
Mass.	116	959	62	882	15	190,820	248,268	889,731	1,512,613
N.Y.	446	4,700	709	3,805	186	1,526,434	1,078,893	2,310,674	4,830,425

U.S. 9th Census, III, 416, 426, 478, 479, 480.

Woolen Textile 1880

Cal.	9	708	108	19	1,676,500	334,318	997,539	1,634,858
Mass.	167	13,146	8,210	2,265	24,680,782	7,457,115	27,839,583	45,099,203
N.Y.	159	3,311	2,123	691	8,266,878	1,774,143	6,212,835	9,874,973

Boot and Shoe 1880

Cal. I	535	2,704	189	101	1,296,685	1,303,426	2,351,470	4,581,099
II	81	2,246	165	88	1,001,183	1,064,938	2,022,487	3,649,551
Mass.	1,311	47,548	13,406	1,297	21,275,932	25,204,331	60,217,152	96,686,110
N.Y.	2,831	12,957	3,847	704	8,283,244	6,591,835	13,800,951	24,911,983

Tobacco

Cal.	176	3,238	110	203	1,831,503	956,639	2,060,275	3,947,353
N.Y.	1,683	13,098	5,039	995	8,274,917	7,671,831	11,942,043	24,767,504

Men's Clothing 1880

Cal.	146	1,155	623	21	1,177,604	959,534	2,318,655	3,992,209
Mass.	347	2,740	8,313	214	5,172,043	3,832,244	10,846,464	17,902,662
N.Y.	1,583	36,655	25,822	651	30,517,107	18,374,466	52,712,947	81,133,611

Women's Clothing

Cal.	29	35	633	7	425,270	221,267	660,232	1,152,600
N.Y.	277	1,649	11,892	64	5,141,290	4,196,913	12,577,958	20,314,307

Shirts 1880

Cal.	26	182	173	1	88,300	85,338	154,990	304,850
Mass.	20	66	428	9	150,050	111,519	326,554	564,500
N.Y.	195	1,133	12,453	205	3,732,694	2,730,571	6,410,261	11,014,820

U.S. 10th Census, II, 20, 21, 28, 29, 71, 72, 79, 95, 134.

FOOTNOTES

CHAPTER I

1. For the magnitude of price fluctuations, see Appendix I.
2. Frank Soule, The annals of San Francisco (New York, 1855), 206-207, 212-214, 303, 366-367, 410-413, 418-419.
3. Walter G. Reed, History of Sacramento County (Los Angeles, 1923), 67.
4. San Francisco Bulletin, Dec. 30, 1860.
5. Henry G. Langley, San Francisco Directory 1861-1869.
6. Ibid., 1861, 42; 1863, 37, etc.
7. Charles H. Shinn, Mining camps, a study in American frontier government (New York, 1895), 149.
8. Sacramento Union, June 10, 1851; Merchants' Magazine and Commercial Review (Hunt's Merchants' Magazine) XXVII (Oct. 1852), 383; W. B. Comstock to S. W. Comstock Aug. 1, 1851, in the Comstock Papers in the Baker Library, Harvard Business School.
9. It varies with different kinds of sluices, of course. See Charles Ferguson, The experience of a Forty-niner during thirty years' residence in California and Australia (Cleveland, 1888), 200.
10. Theodore Hittell, History of California (San Francisco, 1897), III, 50-51.
11. San Francisco Bulletin, Mar. 29, 1859.
12. California Senate Journal 1854. Appendix, Doc. 9.
13. Charles H. Shinn, Mining camps, 159; Hittell, History of California, III, 252-258.
14. Hubert H. Bancroft, History of California (San Francisco,

146

1888), VI, 412; Kirk Munroe, "Hydraulic mining in California," Harper's weekly, XXXIX (May 15, 1895), 470; J. Ross Browne and James W. Taylor, Report upon the mineral resources of the United States (Washington, 1867), 186. Estimates vary but the trend was unmistakable.

CHAPTER II, Part I

1. California Senate Journal 1850, Appendix, 493-497. Senate Journal 1850, 591-598.
2. Herbert O. Lang, History of Tuolumne County (San Francisco, 1882), 34, 44-45.
3. L. D. Borthwick. Three Years in California (Oakland, 1948 reprint), 117-118.
4. Ibid., 217-218.
5. Ibid., 118.
6. 1850 Manuscript Population Census.
7. U.S. 1850 Census, 976. The returns from California were far from complete, and part of the returns including that from San Francisco was lost.
8. James O'Meare, "The Chinese in Early Days," in the Overland Monthly. N.S. IV, 5 (May 1889), 477.
9. Hittell, History of California, IV, 102.
10. John W. Davis to John M. Clayton, Canton, China, Feb. 22, 1849, in the National Archives; Labor Contract, in the Wells and Fargo Museum, San Francisco, California.
11. See footnote 18.
12. California Senate Journal, 1852, 168, 306, 307, 669-675.
13. Report of the Joint Special Committee to Investigate Chinese Immigration (44th Congress, 2nd Session, 1876-1877, Senate Report 689), 1196.
14. My own tabulation from 1852 Special Census for California.
15. California Senate Journal, 1852, 373-378.
16. Alta, Apr. 25, Apr. 26, May 14, 1852. Los Angeles Star, Aug. 11, Sept. 3, 1853.
17. Alta, May 15, 1854.
18. Sir Henry Huntley, California; its gold and its population (London, 1856), 250-255; Alta, May 15, 1852.
19. Lucile Eaves, A history of California labor legislation

(Berkeley, Cal., 1910), 118.
20. Sacramento Union, Oct. 30, 1851.
21. Ibid., Apr. 24, 1852.
22. Huntley, California, 252-253.
23. Alta, Feb. 28, 1853.
24. Alta, Feb. 12, Feb. 15, 1853.
25. Sacramento Union, May 3, 1852.
26. Ibid., May 11, 1852.
27. Stephen Williams, Chinese in the California mines, 1848-1860. M.A. thesis, Stanford University.
28. Calaveras Mining Laws 1854-1857, Mss. in the California State Library.
29. California Assembly Journal 1852, 373-378.
30. Ibid., Appendix, 1853, Dec. 28.
31. Ibid., 4-5, 19-20.
32. Nevada City Journal, May 8, 1952.
33. California Assembly Journal 1853, Doc. 28, 15.
34. California Senate Journal, 1852, 67-68.
35. California Statutes 1853, 62-63.
36. Ibid., 1855, 216; California Statutes 1856, 141.
37. California Statutes 1856, 147; California Statutes 1857, 182-183.
38. Appendix to Senate Journal, 1855, Doc. 19, 16.
39. Rosena A. Giles, Shasta County, California, a history (Oakland, Cal., 1949), 61.
40. Bulletin, Jan. 12, 1858.
41. Ibid., July 28, 1858.
42. Ibid., July 7, 1856.
43. Ibid., Oct. 10, 1857; July 28, 1858.
44. Ibid., Dec. 29, 1856.
45. Rodman W. Paul, California gold, the beginning of mining in the Far West (Cambridge, 1947), 350; California mining journal, Feb. 29, 1858; Irving McKee, Alanzo Delano's California correspondence, 24, 90.
46. California mining journal, Feb. 19, 1856.
47. Ibid., July 27, 1857.
48. Ibid., Jan. 14, 1855.
49. California Senate Journal, 1855-1859.
50. Tabulated form Calaveras Mining Laws Mss. deposited in California State Library, Sacramento, California.

51. California Assembly Journal 1853, Doc. 28, 8.
52. Ibid., 10.
53. J.C. Borthwick, Three years in California, 150.

CHAPTER II, Part II

1. San Francisco Mercantile Gazette and Shipping Register, June 4, 1857; Sept. 4, 1857; Feb. 4, 1858; Apr. 3, 1858; May 1 - December 31, 1858.
2. Bulletin, December 1, 1858.
3. Ibid., Jan. 12, 1862.
4. Robert L. Haley, The hydraulic mining controversy in California 1856-1895, a case study of sectionalism. Ph.D. thesis, Stanford University, 1953, 37-38.
5. Ibid., 41.
6. California Senate Journal, 1859-1864.
7. Hereafter only the length and the capacity of the mining ditches were reported.
8. Mining and Scientific Press, Feb. 8, 1961.
9. J. Ross Browne, Report upon mineral resources of states and territories west of the Rocky Mountains (Washington, 1868), 181.
10. See Appendix II.
11. U.S. Eighth Census, I, 611-615.
12. U.S. Ninth Census, I, 722.
13. California Senate Journal, 1860-1864.
14. Ibid., 1864-1869.
15. The tax figures indicate that more than 15,000 Chinese left the mines between 1865 and 1868. Because the difficulties in the collection of taxes during depression, an allowance for exaggeration as to the enormity of the exodus must be made. In all probability 10,000 would be closer to the truth.

CHAPTER II, Part III

1. Mining and Scientific Press, Jan. 20, 1877.
2. See Appendix II.
3. U.S. Ninth Census, III, 150.
4. U.S. 1860 Manuscript Products of Industry Census, in the

California State Library, Sacramento, Cal.

5. 1860 Manuscript Population Census. (In microfilm)
6. Mining and Scientific Press, Nov. 23, 1867; Sept. 24, 1881.
7. Rossiter Raymond, Statistics of mines and mining in the states and territories west of the Rocky Mountains, 1868 (Washington, 1869), 54, 55; Statistics of mines and mining 1870, 2-3; Mining and Scientific Press, Aug. 6, 1861.
8. Mining and Scientific Press, Aug. 6, 1871.
9. Alta, May 24, 1869.
10. Bulletin, Jan. 6, 1871.
11. Mining and Scientific Press, July 8, 1871.
12. Raymond, Statistics of mines and mining 1870, 2-3.
13. Black Bear Mining Company wage ledger, Mss. in the California State Historical Society, San Francisco, Cal. See also footnote 21.
14. Allen Nevins, Fremont, the West's greatest adventurer (New York, 1928), II, 525.
15. Bulletin, Oct. 27, 1857.
16. Ibid.
17. Raymond, Statistics of mines and mining 1870, 4.
18. Bancroft scrapbooks, LI: I, 146. Bancroft manuscript in the Bancroft Library.
19. Raymond, Statistics of mines and mining, 1870, 21, 67, 79. $4 for the skilled and $3 daily for the unskilled; other counties, 27, 31, 35, 38, 40, 54, 61, 67, 70, 72-73, 79, 82, 83.
20. Ibid., 31.
21. Ibid., 5; Black Bear Mining Company wage ledger; Hermitage Mining Company wage book, Mss. in the Baker Libr., El Dorado Water and Deep Gravel Mining Company wage book, Mss. in the Huntington Libr., San Marino, Cal.
22. Raymond, Statistics of mines and mining, 1870, 5.
23. El Dorado Water and Deep Gravel Mining Company wage ledger. Other sources reported slightly higher wages. (San Francisco Chronicle, Apr. 5, 1876)
24. Black Bear Mining Company wage ledger; Charles C. Haley, Gold placers of California (California State Mining Bureau Bulletin No. 92, San Francisco, 1923), 61; Mining and Scientific Press, Jan. 19, 1878.

25. Raymond, <u>Statistics of mines and mining</u>, 1870, 4.
26. North San Juan <u>Times</u>, July 15, 1876.
27. El Dorado Water and Deep Gravel Co. wage book.
28. <u>North Bloomfield Gravel Mining Company annual report to the stock-holders 1875</u> (San Francisco, 1875), 19-26; <u>Annual report 1879</u>, 28.
29. <u>Ibid.</u>
30. <u>Annual report of Amador Mining Company 1870</u> (San Francisco, 1870), 13.
31. <u>Ibid.</u>, 13-16. Raymond, <u>Statistics of mines and mining</u>, 1873, 93; <u>North Bloomfield annual report 1880</u>, 14.
32. If the mining companies' wage books examined are typical.
33. <u>North Bloomfield Gravel Mining Company annual report to the stockholders</u>, 1875, 1879, 1881; William Hayne and W.D. Pagan, <u>The North Star Mine</u> (Grass Valley, 1918), 6-7, Louis Janin, <u>Report of the Excelsior Water and Mining Company</u>, Smartville, California (San Francisco, 1879), 12, 14.
34. Farlet Judson, "The Yuba Hydraulic Mines" in the <u>Overland Monthly</u>, V (1870) 221.
35. Edward Vischer, "A trip to the mining region in the spring of 1859," in <u>The Quarterly of the California Historical Society</u>, XI, 2 (June, 1952), 228.
36. My own tabulation from 1870 and 1880 manuscript census.
37. Sun Sun Wo Company account book, 1874, in the California State Historical Society, San Francisco, California; Ewong Tai Wo Company account book, 1870-1912, in the Bancroft Library. Foundation Mining Company account book, in the California State Library.
38. Monterey <u>Gazette</u>, Apr. 6, 1886.

CHAPTER III

1. According to its account books deposited in the M.H. De Young Museum, San Francisco, Cal., it was open to traffic on May 20, 1858. It was under construction in 1856. John C. Fremont had built a four-mile track with Chinese labor in the 1850's. Reuben L. Underhill, <u>From cowhide to golden fleece, 1852-1858</u> (Stanford, 1939), 214.

2. Alta, Apr. 12, 1862.
3. Bancroft, History of California, VII, 145; Annie D. Coulter, The economic aspects of the Chinese labor problem. M.A. thesis, University of California, 1902, 24.
4. Even Henry H. Newhall, who was mainly responsible for the introduction of Chinese labor, ignored this episode entirely in his dictations deposited in the Bancroft Library.
5. Report of the Joint Special Committee to Investigate Chinese Immigration, 777.
6. Cerinda W. Evans, Collis P. Huntington (Newport, Va., 1954), 115.
7. W. F. Bailey, The story of the Central Pacific (Pamphlet No. 7, Bancroft Company, San Francisco, 1881), 212; Report of the chief engineer upon surveys and progress of construction of the Central Pacific Railroad of California (Sacramento, Dec. 1865), 16. Subsequent citations: Report of the chief engineer.
8. Evans, Huntington, 125.
9. Report of the special committee, 723.
10. Edwin Sabin, Building the Pacific Railroad (Philadelphia, 1919), 110.
11. Clark, Leland Stanford, 215.
12. United States Pacific Railway Commission, Testimony taken by the commission, VII, 3665. Subsequent citations: Testimony taken by the commission.
13. Oscar Lewis, The Big Four (New York, 1951), 70-71.
14. Bailey, Central Pacific, 204.
15. Testimony taken by the commission, VII, 3660.
16. Grass Valley Union, Apr. 9, 1867.
17. Report of Special Committee, 727.
18. Alta, Nov. 16, 1867.
19. Sabin, Pacific Railroad, 120.
20. Testimony taken by the commission, VII, 3659; Report of special committee, 724.
21. Alta, Nov. 16, 1867.
22. Testimony taken by the commission, VI, 3226.
23. Alta, July 1; July 3, 1867.
24. Mariposa Gazette, July 13, 1867.
25. Alta, July 1, 1867.

26. Report of special committee, 669.
27. Alta, July 3, 1867.
28. San Francisco Commercial Herald and Market Review, July 11, 1867.
29. Treasury Department, Report of the Internal Commerce of the United States for the year 1890, 51st Congress, 2nd Session, 1890-1891, House Executive Doc. 6), 1162.
30. Pioneer, "What railroad has done for California," in the Ben Truman Scrap book on Pacific Railroads, Vol. B, in the Los Angeles Museum.
31. Report of special committee, 721-723.
32. Ibid., 600, 603.
33. Report of special committee, 721.
34. U.S. Tenth Census, I, 401.
35. U.S. Ninth Census, I, 711; 1868 figures are my own estimates based on Foreign Miners' Tax receipt.
36. Report of Secretary of Treasury on commerce and trade, 1869-1881.
37. For freight rates see Wholesale price, wages, and transportation, Report by Mr. Aldrich from the Committee of Finance March 3, 1893 (52nd Congress, 2nd Session, Senate Report No. 1394), I. Table 117, pp. 593-609.
38. Population from about 500,000 in 1870 to 860,000 in 1880, volume of import from 500,000 tons to 860,000 tons.
39. Treasury Department, Report of the internal commerce of the United States for the year 1890, 151.

CHAPTER IV

1. Computed from figures in Appendix IV.
2. Bulletin, Jan. 5, 1867.
3. Alta., Jan. 11, Jan. 16, Feb. 13, Feb. 24, Mar. 14, Apr. 5, 1867.
4. Ibid., Mar. 7, 1867.
5. Thomas Malone, The Democratic party in California 1865-1868, 68. Manuscript M.A. thesis, Stanford, 1949.
6. Bulletin, Jan. 9, 1868.
7. Ibid., Mar. 7, 1867.
8. Winfield David, History of political conventions in

<u>California 1849-1892</u> (Sacramento, 1895), 29; <u>Alta</u>, Mar.
1, 1867; <u>Bulletin,</u> Jan. 14, Feb. 20, Feb. 21, 1867.

9. <u>Bulletin</u>, July 12, Aug. 24, 1870.

10. <u>Ibid.</u>, Jan. 13, 1874.

11. <u>Aldrich Report</u>, 1. Table 117, pp. 593-609.

12. Wesley C. Mitchell, <u>Gold, prices, and wages under the Greenback system</u> (Berkeley, 1908), 4-5, 23-24.

13. San Francisco Board of Supervisors, <u>San Francisco munici-ple report</u>, 1874-1881.

14. <u>United States Tenth Census</u>, I, 811, 821, 839, 841, 828.

15. John S. Hittell, <u>Commerce and industries</u>, 112.

16. <u>Ibid.</u>, 111.

17. <u>Ibid</u>.

18. <u>Report of the Joint Special Committee to Investigate Chinese Immigration</u> (44th Congress, 2d Session, 1876-1877, Senate Report No. 689), 616-617. Subsequent citations: <u>Report of Special Committee</u>.

19. <u>Ibid.</u>, 617-618.

20. <u>Ibid.</u>, 618.

21. H. J. Teschenscher to William Appleton, March 6, Apr. 6, July 31, Sept. 30, Oct. 31, Dec. 31, 1849. Appleton Papers, in the Baker Library. Harvard Business School.

22. <u>Bulletin</u>, May 27, 1858.

23. <u>Alta</u>, May 2, 1853; Frank Soule, <u>Annals of San Francisco</u> (New York, 1855), 459.

24. For instance, between 1850 and 1862 there were six major floods in Sacramento alone. See Thompson and West, Publisher, <u>History of Sacramento County, California</u> (1880, Oakland).

25. <u>Bulletin</u>, Apr. 5, 1876.

26. <u>Ibid.</u>

27. <u>Report of special committee,</u> 614, 670, 687, 709, 822. Therefore, they argued, there was no need to regulate Chinese immigration by law.

28. <u>Ibid.</u>, 1176-1177. There are slight discrepancies in figures cited by Alfred Wheeler and Augustus Loomis, though both based on the same source.

29. <u>Ibid</u>.

30. My own calculation based on receipts of Foreign Miner's Tax.

31. My own estimates.
32. Ibid.
33. U.S. Eleventh Census, 1, 401.
34. My own count from 1880 Manuscript Population Census.

CHAPTER V, Part I

1. Bancroft, History of California, VI, 542-562.
2. Computed by dividing the total value of farmland by the total acreage of improved land from figures in 1850 Census, 20, 1880 Agricultural Census, 6, 9, 12, 13, 16.
3. Ibid.
4. 1880 Agricultural Census, 25.
5. Ibid.
6. Alta, July 1, 1854.
7. Los Angeles Evening Express, Apr. 3, 1877; May 17, 1878.
8. L.J. Rose to Henry D.Bacon, Sept. 1, 1880. In this letter Rose informed Bacon that because of a market agreement between a certain Mr. Shorb and himself, he could no longer purchase the grapes of the Bacon vineyard, which was located at Mr. Shorb's territory. Furthermore he stated that they would not pay more than $1.00 per hundred pounds of Mission grapes. In the Bacon papers.
9. Frank Page Bacon to H.D. Bacon Sept. 24, 1880. In this letter F.P. Bacon stated that L.J. Rose agreed to purchase their grapes and at a much higher price than indicated in his letter dated Sept. 1.
10. Department of Agriculture, Report of the Commissioner of Agriculture for the year 1870 (Washington, 1871), 567.
11. Claude B. Hutchinson, California agriculture (Berkeley, 1946), 445.
12. Victor M. Cone, Irrigation in the San Joaquin Valley, California (United States Department of Agriculture, Office of Experiment Station, Bulletin 239, Washington, 1911), 22, 26.
13. Ibid., 23.
14. "Fresh water tide land of California" (San Francisco, 1864), 2; in California Pamphlets, IX; "Irrigation in California, the San Joaquin and Tulare plains" (Sacramento, 1872), 2; in the California Pamphlets IX, in the Bancroft Library.

15. Report of special committee, 437.
16. H.D. Bacon Business Papers, in the Huntington Libr.
17. Ibid., Nov. 4, 1875.
18. Report of the State Board of Agriculture for the year 1874 (Sacramento, 1875), 311.
19. Report of special committee, 436-437.
20. My own tabulation from the Manuscript Population Census.

CHAPTER V, Part II

1. 1860 Manuscript Agricultural Census, in the California State Library.
2. 1870 Manuscript Agricultural Census, in the California State Library.
3. Ibid., Sacramento County.
4. 1880 Manuscript Agricultural Census, San Joaquin County.
5. Report of special congressional committee, 440.
6. My own tabulation from the 1860, 1870, and 1880 Manuscript Population Census. 1870 figures included farm operators only. There were 296 Chinese farm laborers under the employment of Chinese farmers.
7. 1880 Manuscript population census.
8. My own tabulation from the 1860, 1870, and 1880 Manuscript Population Census.
9. Los Angeles, Sacramento, San Joaquin, and Yuba County Assessment Rolls, deposited in the County Court Houses in Los Angeles, Sacramento, Stockton, and Marysville respectively. The following years had been examined: 1852, 1855, 1858, 1860, 1862, 1865, 1868, 1870, 1872, 1875, 1878, and 1880.
10. 1870,1880 Manuscript Population Census, Tehema County.
11. My own tabulation from the Manuscript Population Census of 1870 and 1880.
12. 1880 Manuscript Population Census.
13. Post, Sept. 6, 1877.
14. My own tabulation from the 1870 Manuscript Population Census.
15. Call, Aug. 20, 1877.
16. Sacramento County Assessment Rolls 1878, County Court

House, Sacramento, California.   One of the ranchers leased 7, 304 acres of land.

17. <u>Call</u>, Aug. 20, 1877.
18. My own tabulation from the 1860 Manuscript Population Census.
19. <u>U. S. Ninth Census,</u> I, 722. <u>U. S. Tenth Census</u>, I, 811. Figures for the Chinese are my own count from the Manuscript Population Census of 1870 and 1880.
20. <u>Ibid</u>.
21. <u>Post</u>, Sept. 6, 1877.

CHAPTER V, Part III

1. <u>Pacific Rural Press</u>, V (Aug. 2, 1873), 76.
2. California. The Governor's Commission to Survey the Agricultural resources of the San Joaquin Valley, <u>Agricultural labor in the San Joaquin Valley, recommendations and preliminary report</u> (Sacramento, 1950), 12.
3. Claude B. Hutchinson, <u>The need for seasonal labor in relation to the size of farm in California</u> (Berkeley, 1945), 3.
4. <u>Ibid.</u>, wage books, 1859-1880.
5. <u>Ibid.</u>, Indian books (Indian wage books) 1859-1865.
6. Carosso, <u>California wine industry</u>, 71.
7. B. D. Wilson Papers Sept. 9, Oct. 2, 1864. In the Wilson papers, Huntington Library.
8. <u>Report of special committee</u>, 573.
9. <u>Transactions and annual report of the San Joaquin Agricultural Society, third annual report</u> (San Francisco, 1863), (San Francisco, 1863), 170-171.
10. <u>Alta</u>, Nov. 4, 1877.
11. Carosso, <u>California wine industry</u>, 71.
12. <u>California State Agricultural Society Transactions 1866-1867</u>, 447.
13. <u>California Agricultural Society</u> Transactions 1872, 257-8; <u>Alta</u>, July 2, 1869.
14. The Henry Dalton Papers, wage book, 1870-1880.
15. Frank Page Bacon to H. D. Bacon,Sept. 14, 1877.
16. <u>California Agricultural Society Transactions 1872</u>, 307.
17. My own count from the Manuscript Population Census of

1870 and 1880.

18. U.S. Ninth Census, 1, 722. U.S. Tenth Census, 2, 811.
19. 1880 Manuscript Agricultural Census.
20. Harry Schwartz, Seasonal farm labor in the United States with special reference to hired worker in fruit and vegetable, and sugar-beet production (New York, 1954), 68.
21. 1880 Manuscript Agricultural Census, San Joaquin County.
22. Computed from 1880 Manuscript Agricultural Census, Los Angeles County.
23. Ibid., San Joaquin County.
24. The Blucher Ranch Business Papers, in the M.H. De Young Museum, San Francisco, Cal.
25. My own calculations from reports of San Francisco Labor Exchange in S.F. Bulletin 1868-1880.
26. Report of special committee, 439.
27. Alta, Jan. 27, 1868.
28. Marysville Weekly Appeal, Feb. 20, 1869; Mar. 29, 1875.
29. Ibid., 1067.
30. Ibid., 1091.
31. Post, Sept. 3, 1877.
32. Sacramento Bee-Union, Apr. 4, 1877.
33. Alta, Sept. 10, 1877.
34. Alta, Nov. 4, 1877.
35. Ibid.
36. Dudley Morehead, Sectionalism and the California constitution of 1879, 316, 333.
37. Pacific Rural Press, XXII (Dec. 24, 1881), 418.

CHAPTER VI, Part I

1. Alta, Apr. 6, 1867. Bulletin, May 6, 1867.
2. Computed from Wholesale prices, wages, and transportation, Report by Mr. Aldrich from the Committee of Finance March 3, 1893 (52nd Congress, 2nd Session, Senate Report 1394), I, 82.
3. San Francisco municipal report, 1867-1881.
4. Hittell, Commerce and industries, 109.
5. Alta, May 6, 1867.
6. A.G. Loomis, "How our Chinamen were employed," in the

7. Report of special committee, 607.
8. Ibid.
9. Ibid., 613.
10. Ibid., 608.
11. Ibid., 554, 608, 613.
12. Ibid. John S. Hittel, Replies to printed queries on manu-
    factures, Mss. in the Bancroft Collection, Bancroft Library.
13. Ibid. Pacific Rural Press, VII (Apr. 11, 1874), 229.
14. First annual report of the Commissioner of Labor, March
    1886 (Washington, 1886), 391-392.

CHAPTER VI, Part II

1. Bancroft, History of California, VII, 89.
2. L. Neville Rieman, The men's suit industry (Boston, 1947),
    10.
3. U.S. Ninth Census, II, 497.
4. Post, Sept. 1, 1877.
5. San Francisco municipal report, 1870-1881.
6. Post, Sept. 5, 1877.
7. Ibid., Sept. 6, 1877.
8. Post, Aug. 20, 1877.
9. Post, Aug. 31, 1877.
10. Post, Aug. 20, 1877.
11. Post, Sept. 5, 1877.
12. Ibid.
13. Post, Aug. 31; Sept. 5, 1877.
14. If we compute from census figures as reproduced in Ap-
    pendix V, the gross income-variable cost ratios for Cali-
    fornia's clothing industries are slightly higher than those
    of New York.
15. U.S. Ninth Census, II, 497.
16. See notations by the census taker in the Manuscript Manu-
    facturing Census of 1880.
17. 1880 Manuscript Manufacture Census.
18. John S. Hittell, Commerce and Industries, 454.
19. Report of special committee, 252.
20. Ottis Gibson, Chinese in America (San Francisco, 1877),
    59.

21. My own tabulation from 1880 Manuscript Census, <u>San Francisco Journal of Commerce</u>, Mar. 20, 1879, estimated there were 1,300 workers in clothing industry, of whom about 1,000 were Chinese.
22. Computed from data in Appendix V.
23. <u>Post</u>, Aug. 11, 1877.
24. <u>San Francisco municipal report</u>, 1872-1881.
25. <u>Report of special committee</u>, 244-245.
26. 1870 Manuscript Products of Industry Census.
27. 1880 Manuscript Manufacture Census.
28. <u>Ibid</u>.
29. <u>Ibid</u>.
30. Hittell, <u>Commerce and industries</u>, 458.
31. <u>Post</u>, Aug. 31, 1877.
32. Hittell, <u>Commerce and industries</u>, 456.

CHAPTER VII, Part I

1. Blanche Hazard, <u>The organization of the boot and shoe industry in Massachusetts before 1875</u> (Cambridge, 1921), 99-101.
2. <u>San Francisco municipal report</u>, 1870-1881.
3. <u>Call</u>, Apr. 11, 1873.
4. <u>Wholesale prices, wages and transportation reported by Mr. Aldrich from the Committee of Finance</u> (52nd Congress, 2nd Session, Senate Report 1394), I, 79, 82; Wesley Mitchell, <u>Gold, prices, and wages</u>, 9, 13.
5. <u>Report of special committee</u>, 335, 1211.
6. <u>Bulletin</u>, Sept. 1, 1876.
7. <u>First annual report of the Commissioner of Labor</u>, 391.
8. Buckingham and Hecht Mss. in the Bancroft Library; <u>Bulletin</u>, May 29, 1870.
9. Hazard, <u>Boots and shoe industry</u>, 121.
10. <u>First annual report of the Commissioner of Labor</u>, 391.
11. <u>Ibid</u>.
12. <u>U.S. Ninth Census</u>, I, 799.
13. <u>U.S. Eighth Census</u>, II, 35-36.
14. <u>Alta</u>, Apr. 6, 1867.
15. Computed from figures in Appendix V.

16. _Ibid._
17. Computed from 1870 Manuscript Products of Industry Census.
18. _Ibid._
19. Hazard, B., _Boot and shoe industry,_ 150.
20. _Bulletin,_ Feb. 26, 1873.
21. _Call,_ Apr. 11, 1873.
22. _Post,_ Sept. 1, 1877.
23. _San Francisco municipal reports;_ 1880 Manuscript Manufacture Census in the California State Library.
24. _Report of special committee,_ 339.
25. _Ibid._
26. _Ibid.,_ 1221.
27. _Ibid._; they cannot be located in San Francisco _Directories_ after 1878.
28. _Ibid._
29. _U.S. Tenth Census,_ II, 20-21.
30. _San Francisco Directory,_ 1876-1880.
31. See figures in Appendix V.
32. Computed from 1880 Manuscript Manufacture Census.
33. _Ibid._
34. _Ibid._
35. _Ibid._
36. Tabulated from 1880 Manuscript Population Census.
37. Tabulated and computed from 1880 Manuscript Manufacture Census.
38. _Ibid._
39. _Ibid._
40. _U.S. Tenth Census,_ II, 448.
41. 1880 Manuscript Manufacture Census.
42. _Report of special committee,_ 18.
43. Computed from 1870 Manuscript Products of Industry Census.
44. _Ibid._
45. _San Francisco municipal report,_ 1870-1881.
46. Computed from 1880 Manuscript Manufacture Census.
47. Shoe manufacturing in Lynn, Massachusetts, consisted of 33 distinct processes in the 1870's. See Hazard, _Boot and shoe industry,_ 120-121.

CHAPTER VII, Part II

1. _Bulletin_, Nov. 3, 1859.
2. _San Francisco Directory 1867_, 98.
3. _Alta_, Feb. 4, 1867; see also San Francisco _Mercantile Gazette and Price Current_, Jan. 9, 1866.
4. _Bulletin_, 1860-1870.
5. Willis N. Baer, _The economic development of cigar industry in the United States_ (Lancaster, Pa., 1930), 105.
6. _San Francisco municipal report_, 1867-1881.
7. Baer, _Cigar industry_, 81.
8. _Ibid._, 91.
9. _S.F. Directory_, 1867, 98.
10. _U.S. 1870 Census_, 799.
11. Computed from 1870 Manuscript Manufacture Census.
12. _Ibid._
13. _Ibid._
14. _San Francisco municipal report_, 1871-1881. Figures vary from year to year, and the lists in the municipal report and census do not match.
15. Computed from 1880 Manuscript Manufacture Census, by dividing the total wage by daily wage rate times number of workers with adjustment in regard to temporary labor force.
16. _Ibid._
17. _Ibid._
18. _Ibid._
19. _Ibid._
20. _Ibid._
21. _Ibid._
22. _Post_, Nov. 13, 1877.
23. _First annual report of the Commissioner of Labor_, March 1886, 417.
24. _Second biennial report of the Bureau of Labor Statistics of California_ (Sacramento, 1888), 139.
25. _U.S. Ninth Census_, I, 722.
26. My own tabulation from 1880 Manuscript Population Census.
27. _Ibid._
28. _Bulletin_, Feb. 20, 1880; H.H. Bancroft, _Essay and Miscellany_ (San Francisco, 1890), 349-350.

29. My own tabulation from 1880 Manuscript Population Census.
30. The writer failed to arrange an interview with one of the decendents of one of the well known contractors. Other Chinese informants were unable to furnish specific details.
31. Bancroft Scrap VI, 365-367. In Bancroft Library.
32. Report of special committee, 674.
33. Mariposa Gazette, Mar. 18, 1876.

CHAPTER VIII

1. Report of the Joint Special Committee to Investigate Chinese Immigration (44th Congress, 2nd Session, 1876-1877, Senate Report No. 689), 564. Because of their repetitious nature, anti- or pro-Chinese arguments can be documented almost exclusively from this source.
2. Ibid., 608.
3. Ibid., 801. As one employer explained his reason for substituting Chinese for white labor: "When we started six years ago we had a better price for our goods and could afford it; but the price has been so terribly reduced by importation that we were compelled either to change off and compete or quit; and the moment we quit the white help would have quit also."
4. Ibid., 574, 1201.
5. Ibid., 568.
6. Alta, July 31, 1876.
7. Report of special committee, 400, 541, 554, 667, 668.
8. Ibid., 527.
9. Layres, Augustus, Friends of right, justice, and humanity, or the other side of the Chinese question (San Francisco, 1886), 14.
     Professor Hamilton seems to hold the same opinion, in his analysis of the relationships between wage and the rise of capitalism in England, France and Spain. Earl J. Hamilton, "Price as a factor in business growth," Journal of economic history, XII, 4 (Fall, 1952), 325-349.
10. Bulletin, Feb. 20, 1867.
11. Report of special committee, 1201.
12. Ibid., 1081.

13. _Ibid._, 367. "If no Chinese had come to California, it is my judgment that our trades and manufactures would have grown a little slower than they have; that some people would have made less money than they have, but that they would have grown, and to the present extent, with white labor; and they may have been less remunerative to some of the capitalists, they would have been remunerative to the laborers. Just as much money would have been made, but it would have been distributed among the laboring or working men than it is now."

14. _Ibid._, 369. "There is no doubt that the European immigrant, however poor he may be, immediately takes a position in society, so far as comforts and home are concerned, and brings about him all the refinement, and educates his children, and clothes himself up to the fullest possibility of their [sic] earnings."

15. _Ibid._, 1089.

16. _Ibid._, 348. "We have been in a very bad condition from the fact that business is very dull, and the workingmen imagine that that is to a great extent owing to the large number of Chinamen coming here, because by destroying or rather reducing our wage it certainly must destroy our power of consumption, and the retail dealers eventually will be sufferers as well as we. Hence the general depression in our midst."

17. _Ibid._, 959.

18. _Ibid._, 250, 257, 350.

19. _San Francisco Directory_ 1876-1877. (pages not numbered)

20. _Argonaut_, II (Jan. 1878), 8. "If there had been no Chinese upon this coast. . .riches would have been more evenly distributed, and California would be the exceptional spot upon God's footstool where there had been no hard times, and where poverty and destitution are forever impossible."; Chico _Chronical-Record_, Jan. 11, 1871.

SELECTED BIBLIOGRAPHY

DOCUMENTS

United States

Bureau of Labor, _First annual report of the Commissioner of Labor Mar. 1886: industrial depression_.

Census Bureau. _United States Census._ 1850-1890.

_____. Manuscript Population Census, 1850-1880. (In microfilm).

_____. Manuscript Agriculture Census, 1860-1880, in the California State Library, Sacramento, Cal.

_____. Manuscript Manufacture Census, 1860-1880. (Title varies), in the California State Library.

Department of Agriculture. _Monthly report of the Department of Agriculture,_ May 1863-Dec. 1876.

_____. _Report of the Commissioner of Agriculture,_ 1863-1880. (Title varies).

Treasury Department. _Annual report and statements of the Chief of the Bureau of Statistics on Commerce and Navigation,_ 1850-1882. (Title varies).

_____. _Report of the internal commerce of the United States for the year 1890._ (51st Congress, 2nd Session, House Executive Document No. 6.)

United States Pacific Railway Commission. _Testimony taken by the Commission._

Report of the Joint Special Committee to Investigate Chinese Immigration (44th Congress, 2nd Session, Report No. 689).

Retail prices and wages, reported by Mr. Aldrich from the Committee on Finance, July 19, 1892. (52nd Congress, 1st Session, Senate Report No. 986.)

Wholesale Prices, wages, and transportation, reported by Mr. Aldrich from the Committee on Finance, Mar. 1893. (52nd Congress, 2nd Session, Senate Report No. 1394.)

CALIFORNIA

Annual report of the Board of Bank Commissioners of the State of California, 1879-1882.

Annual report of the Board of the State Viticultural Commissioners, 1880-1887.

Annual report of the State Minerologist, 1880-1882.

Appendix to Journals of Assembly and Senate, 1855-1880.

Assembly Journal, 1850-1880.

Biennial report of the Bureau of Labor Statistics of California, 1883-1900.

Biennial report of the Commission of Horticulture of the State of California, 1903-1908.

Biennial report of the State Board of Horticulture, 1881-1884.

California Statutes, 1850-1880.

Report of the State Board of Agriculture, 1861-1880.

Senate Journal, 1850-1880.

LOCAL

Los Angeles County Assessment Rolls. In County Auditor's Office, Los Angeles, California.

Sacramento County Assessment Rolls. In the County Court House, Sacramento, California.

San Joaquin County Assessment Rolls. In the County Court House, Stockton, California.

San Francisco Board of Supervisors. San Francisco municipal report, 1859-1881.

Yuba County Assessment Rolls. In the County Court House, Marysville, California.

BOOKS AND MONOGRAPHS

Averill, Charles V. Placer mining for gold in California. Division of Mines, San Francisco, Bulletin No. 135, Oct. 1940.

Baer, Willis N. The economic development of cigar industry in the United States. Lancaster, Pa. 1930.

Bailey, W. F. The story of the Central Pacific. San Francisco 1881.

Bancroft, Hubert H. California Inter Pocula. San Francisco. 1888.

_____. Chronicles of the builders of the commonwealth. San Francisco, 1891.

_____. Essay and miscellany. San Francisco, 1890.

_____. History of California, San Francisco, 1884-1890.

Borthwick, J. D. Three years in California. Oakland, Cal. 1948 reprint.

Bowie, Augustus J., Jr. Hydraulic mining in California. Easton, Pa. 1878.

Brown, Amos. Report on the properties and domain of the California Water Company, situated on Georgetown Divide; embracing the mining, water, and land resources of the country between the South and Middle Fork of the American River in El Dorado, California. San Francisco, 1874.

Browne, J. Ross. Report of J. Ross Browne on mineral resources of the states and territories west of the Rocky Mountains,

Washington, 1868.

Browne, J. Ross. <u>Resources of the Pacific slope</u>, San Francisco, 1869.

Browne, J. Ross, and Taylor, James W. <u>Report upon the resources of the United States</u>, Washington, 1867.

California. The Governor's Committee to Survey the Agricultural
labor resources of the San Joaquin Valley. <u>Agricultural labor
in the San Joaquin Valley, recommendations and preliminary
report.</u> Sacramento, 1950.

Carosso, Vincent. <u>The California wine industry 1830-1895, a
study of formative years</u>. Berkeley, 1951.

Caughey, John W. <u>Gold is the cornerstone</u>. Berkeley, 1948.

_____. <u>Rushing for gold.</u> Berkeley, 1949.

Clark, George T. <u>Leland Stanford</u>, Stanford, 1921.

Cleland, Robert G., and Hardy, Osgood. <u>March of industry.</u>
Los Angeles, 1929.

Coolidge, Mary R. <u>Chinese immigration.</u> New York, 1909.

Coy, Owen C. <u>California: gold days.</u> San Francisco, 1929.

Cronise, Titus F. <u>The natural wealth of California.</u> San Francisco, 1868.

Cross, Ira B. <u>A history of labor movement in California.</u>
Berkeley, 1910.

_____. <u>Financing an empire: a history of banking in
California.</u> Chicago, 1927.

Eaves, Lucile. <u>A history of California labor legislation.</u>
Berkeley, 1910.

Eldredge, Zoeth S., ed. <u>History of California</u>. New York, 1915.

Evans, Cerinda W. <u>Collis Potter Huntington.</u> Newport, 1954.

Ferguson, Charles. <u>The experience of a Forty-niner during
thirty years' residence in California and Austria.</u> Cleveland,
1888.

Fisher, Lloyd H. The Harvest labor market in California. Cambridge, 1953.

Frost, John. History of the state of California. Augurn, N.Y., 1851.

Gerstaecker, F. W. C. California gold mines. Oakland, 1946.

Gibson, Ottis. Chinese in America. San Francisco, 1877.

Greig, Gertrude B. Seasonal fluctuations in employment in the women's clothing industry in New York. New York, 1949.

Haley, Charles C. Gold placers of California. California State Mining Bureau Bulletin No. 92, San Francisco, 1923.

Hazard, Blanche. The organization of the boot and shoe industry in Massachusetts before 1875. Cambridge, 1921.

Hill, James M. Historical summary of gold, silver, copper, lead, and zinc produced in California 1848-1921. Bureau of Mines, Economic paper No. 3, Washington, 1929.

Hittell, John S. The commerce and industries of the Pacific Coast of North America. San Francisco, 1888.

_____. Resources of California. San Francisco, 1868.

Hittell, Theodore. History of California. San Francisco, 1897.

Huntley, Sir Henry. California: its gold and its population, London, 1856.

Hurt, Elsey. California state government and outline of its administrative organizations from 1850 to 1936. Sacramento, 1936.

Hutchinson, Claude B. , The need for seasonal labor in relation to the size of farm in California. Berkeley, 1940.

Lewis, Oscar, The Big Four. New York, 1938.

Mitchell, Westley C. "Gold, price and wage under the greenback standard," University of California publications in Economics, I (1908).

Nevins, Allen. Fremont, the West's greatest adventurer. New York, 1928.

Paul, Rodman W. California gold, the beginning of mining in the Far West. Cambridge, 1947.

Raymond, Rossiter W. Statistics of mines and mining in the states and territories west of the Rocky Mountains. Washington, 1869-1877. (Title varies)

Rieman, L. Neville. The Men's suit industry. Boston, 1947.

Sandmeyer, Elmer C. The anti-Chinese movement in California. Urbana, Ill., 1939.

Schwartz, Harry. Seasonal farm labor in the United States, with special references to hired workers in fruit and vegetable and sugar-beet production. New York, 1954.

Seward, George F. Chinese immigration, its social and economic aspects. San Francisco, 1881.

Shinn, Charles H. Mining camps, a study in American frontier government. New York, 1895.

Underhill, Reubin L. From cowhide to Golden Fleece: 1852-1858, based upon unpublished correspondence of Thomas Oliver Larkin, trade, developer, promoter, and only American consul. Stanford, 1939.

Wright, Benjamin C. Banking in California 1849-1910. San Francisco, 1910.

ALMANACS AND DIRECTORIES

Alta California Almanac.

Bean, Edwin. Bean's history and directory of Nevada County, California. Nevada City, Cal., 1867.

Knight, William H. Handbook almanac for the Pacific States, San Francisco, 1862-1864.

Langley, Henry G. Pacific Coast business directory, 1867-1874.

Marysville city directory.

Sacramento city directory.

San Francisco city directory.

Wells and Fargo Co.   Directory of Chinese Merchants, San
Francisco and Sacramento.

_____.   Directory of Chinese Business Houses.

PAMPHLETS

Amador Mining Company.   Annual report of Amador Mining
Company. San Francisco, 1870.

Bureaus of News, Development Department Southern Pacific
Railroad Company.   Historical outlines: Southern Pacific
Company. San Francisco, 1933.

Central Pacific Railroad Company.   Statement made to the
President of the United States and the Secretary of the Interior of the progress of the work Oct. 10th, 1868. Sacramento, 1868.

_____.   Report of the Chief engineer upon recent surveys
and progress of construction of the Central Pacific Railroad
of California, 1865-1868. Sacramento, 1865-1868.

Hayne, William and Pagan, W. D. The North Star Mine. Grass
Valley, Cal., 1918.

Janin, Louis.   Report on the Excelsior Water and Mining Company, Smartsville, California. San Francisco, 1879.

The Milton Mining and Water Company.   The Milton Mining
and Water Company balance sheet, 1877. San Francisco,
1877.

North Bloomfield Gravel Mining Company. Annual report to the
Stock-holders, 1874-1881. San Francisco, 1874-1881.

_____.   Financial operations of the company during the
season and year ending Dec. 31st 1880. San Francisco, 1881.

Southern Pacific Railroad Company. Annual report of the Southern Pacific Company for the year ending June 30, 1874.
New York, 1874.

_____. The lands of the Southern Pacific Railroad Company of California with general information on the resources of Southern California. San Francisco, 1850.

(Pamphlets on the Chinese in California are too numerous to be listed here. For an extensive bibliography see Pearl Ng, Writings on the Chinese in California. Unpublished M. A. thesis, in the University of California Library.)

ARTICLES CITED

Davis, Horace. "California breadstuffs," in the Journal of Political Economy, II, 517-535 (Sept. 1893).

Munroe, Kirk. "Hydraulic mining in California," in the Harper's Weekly, XXXIX, 470-471 (May 18, 1895).

Shinn, Charles H. "Cooperation on the Pacific Coast," in the Johns Hopkins Studies in Historical and Political Science, IV, 447-486 (1888).

PERIODICALS

Bulletin of the State Agricultural Society, 1865-1880.

California Historical Society Quarterly, 1922-1954.

California State Grange, Patrons of Husbandry, 1873-1880.

Merchants' Magazine and Commercial Review, 1848-1880.

Mining and Scientific Press, 1860-1881.

Overland Monthly and Out West Magazine, 1868-1886.

Pacific Rural Press, 1871-1881.

Proceedings of the Pacific Coast Branch of the American Historical Association, 1926-1930.

Transactions and Annual Report of the San Joaquin Valley Agricultural Society, 1861-1864

Transactions of California State Agricultural Society, 1862-1880.

NEWSPAPERS

Amador Ledger, 1863-1879.

Auburn Placer Herald, 1869-1880.

Chico Weekly Chronicle-Record, 1853-1858; 1873-1879.
    Weekly Courant, 1865-1867.
    Butte County Press, 1867-1868.
    Weekly Butte Record, 1877-1880.
    Daily Evening Record, 1878-1880.

Crescent City Courier, 1872-1880.

Dutch Flat Enquirer, 1864-1873.

Grass Valley Telegraphy, 1858-59; 1866-1870.
        Union, 1865-1867.

Los Angeles Star, 1851-1859.
        Southern News, 1861-1866.
        Semi-Weekly News, 1867-1868.
        Daily News, 1869-1873.
        Evening Express, 1874-1879.

Mariposa Gazette, 1857, 1864, 1874-1880.

Marysville Daily Appeal, 1860-1863.
        Weekly Appeal, 1864-1880.

Nevada City Journal, 1851-1863.
        Transcript, 1865, 1867, 1869.

North San Juan The Hydraulic Press, 1858-1861.
        Times, 1874-1880.

Placerville Mountain Democrats 1864-1880.
        El Dorado County Republican, 1871-1878; 1880.

Sacramento Union, 1851-1853.
        Bee, 1876-1880.

San Francisco Alta California, 1849-1880.
        Bulletin, 1856-1880.
        Chronicle, 1877-1880.

San Francisco <u>Post</u>
          <u>California Police Gazette</u>, 1859-1869
          <u>Shipping List and Price Current</u>, 1854-1855
          <u>Mercantile Gazette and Shipping Register</u>, 1857-
          1858
          <u>Mercantile Gazette and Price Current</u>, 1861-1867
          <u>Commercial Herald and Market Review</u>, 1867-
          1871; 1876-1881.
          <u>Journal of Commerce</u>, 1876-1879.
          *<u>Oriental: or Tung-Ngai San-Luk</u>, 1854.
          <u>Golden Hill News</u>, 1859.
          <u>Chinese News Weekly</u>, 1874-1875.
          <u>Oriental</u>, 1875-1876.

Stockton <u>Independent</u>, 1861-1880.

Yreka <u>Humboldt Times</u>, 1854-1878.
          <u>Union</u>, 1855-1876; 1878-1880.

UNPUBLISHED THESES

<u>In the University of California (at Berkeley) Library</u>

Allen, Rutillus H. <u>Economic history of agriculture in Monterey
     County, California during the American period.</u> Ph.D. 1934.

Cooper, Margaret A. <u>Land, water, settlement in Kern County,
     California 1850-1890</u>, M.A.

Ellison, Joseph. <u>Federal relations of California, 1846-1869:
     a study of the relation of a frontier community with national
     government.</u> Ph.D. 1923.

Fuller, Levi Varden. <u>The supply of agricultural labor as a fac-
     tor in the evolution of farm organization in California</u>. Ph.D.
     1939.

Hughes, Marshal. <u>The Argonaut mining companies 1848-1850.</u>
     M.A. 1939.

----

*The following four papers were published by the Chinese in
San Francisco.

Klein, Julius.   The development of manufacturing industry in
    California up to 1870.   M.A. 1908.

Margo, Joan. The food supply problem of California gold mines
    1848-1855.   M.A. 1947.

Ng, Pearl. Writings on the Chinese in California. M.A., 1939.

In the Stanford University Library

Haley, Robert L.   The hydraulic mining controversy in Cali-
    fornia 1856-1895: a case study of sectionalism. Ph.D. 1953.

Malone, Thomas.   The Democratic Party in California 1865-
    1868. M.A. 1949.

Moorehead, Dudley T. Sectionalism and California Constitution
    of 1879.   Ph.D. 1941.

Reynolds, Charles N.   Oriental, white race relation in Santa
    Clara County, Ph.D. 1927.

Williams, Stephen.   Chinese in California mines 1848-1860.
    M.A.

MANUSCRIPTS

In the Bancroft Library, University of California at Berkeley.

Bancroft Scrapbooks (Hubert Howe Bancroft).

Biographies, dictations, and statements of eminent Californians.

Davis Scrapbooks (Horace Davis).

Hittell Manuscript. (John S. Hittell)

Hittell Scrapbooks (Theodore Hittell).

Chung Tai Co. account books.

Kwong Tai We Co. account books.

Tai Chong Co. account books.

Wing Tai Co. account books.

In the Baker Library, Harvard Business School

William Appleton Papers, in the Dexter collection.

Comstock Papers.

S. Griffiths Morgan Papers.

Hermitage Mining Company wage book. (El Dorado County, California)

In the California State Historical Society, San Francisco, California

Black Bear Mining Company wage book.

Sun Sun Wo Co. account book.

In the California State Library, Sacramento, California

Calaveras Mining Laws.

Delphine Copper Mine account book.

Foundation Mining Company account book.

Taylor and Swerer account book.

Account books. (A country store in San Diego, California)

Account books.   (A country store in Placerville, El Dorado County, California)

In the Huntington Library, San Marino, California

Bacon Papers.   (Henry Douglass Bacon)

El Dorado Water and Deep Gravel Mining Company wage book.